Microprogrammable
Computer
Architectures

ELSEVIER COMPUTER SCIENCE LIBRARY

Computer Design and Architecture Series
EDWARD J. McCLUSKEY, *Editor*

COMPUTER DESIGN AND ARCHITECTURE SERIES

Microprogrammable Computer Architectures

Alan B. Salisbury
U.S. Army Electronics Command

ELSEVIER · NEW YORK
NEW YORK · AMSTERDAM · OXFORD

ELSEVIER NORTH-HOLLAND, INC.
52 Vanderbilt Avenue, New York, NY 10017

ELSEVIER SCIENTIFIC PUBLISHING COMPANY
335 Jan Van Galenstraat, P.O. Box 211
Amsterdam, The Netherlands

Third Printing, 1977

Library of Congress Cataloging in Publication Data

Salisbury, Alan B
    Microprogrammable computer architectures.

    (Computer design and architecture series ; 1)
(Elsevier computer science library)
    Bibliography: p.
    Includes index.
    1. Electronic digital computers. 2. Microprogramm-
ing. I. Title.
QA76.5.S1995   001.6'4'044   75-26337
ISBN 0-444-00175-1
ISBN 0-444-00174-3 pbk.

Manufactured in the United States of America

To Betty, Florence, and Kathy
Yesterday, Today, and Tomorrow

Contents

Preface

This book provides an introduction to the architecture of micro-programmable computers. The term *microprogrammable* as used herein implies machines with writable control store (or otherwise supported for microprogramming by the user) and intended for general purpose microprogramming. This is in contrast to micro-programmed machines employing read-only memories that have been designed only to implement a particular machine language and architecture and are not intended for further microprogramming.

The first chapter provides an historical overview of microprogramming tracing the evolution of the microprogrammable computer. Chapters 2 and 3 develop a comprehensive framework and descriptive parameters for the analysis of microprogrammable computer architectures. The emphasis is on identifying and analyzing those architectural features that provide flexibility and thus enhance the general purpose capabilities of microprogrammable processors. Special attention is also paid to features that have utility in emulation.

The remainder of the book is devoted to case studies of micropro-grammable machine architectures. Four chapters (4 through 7) provide relatively detailed descriptions of particular machines with significantly different architectural concepts (Microdata 3200, Interdata 8/32, Burroughs B1700, and Nanodata QM-1); while in no way exhaustive, these descriptions do cover the salient and most significant features of primary interest from an architectural viewpoint. The final chapter provides brief overview descriptions of an additional six machines (Control Data 5600, Digital Scientific META 4, HP 2100/21MX, Varian 73, Intel 3000, and Western Digital MCP 1600) chosen to round out the variety of architectures presented and in recognition of their popularity or potential. The Intel 3000 and the Western Digital MCP 1600, in particular, are included as representatives of the new breed of microprogrammable microprocessors.

This book does not purport to be a text on microprogramming or computer architecture. Nevertheless, it can serve as a useful reference or supplemental text for a range of courses and seminars. The material presented is largely an outgrowth of research conducted at Stanford University; the reports on which the book is based have already been used as supplemental reading at a number of institutions.

The reader is assumed to have a knowledge of basic machine structure including a familiarity with machine or assembly language programming. Within these constraints, the material will be of interest to computer engineers, computer scientists, programmers, and managers alike.

The author is indebted to many people for helping make this book possible. In particular, E. J. McCluskey, professor of Electrical Engineering and Computer Science at Stanford University and editor of the Computer Design and Architecture Series, is to be credited for encouraging the project and for his careful editing of the manuscript through several rewrites. Thanks also to A. J. Nichols of American Microsystems for his review and constructive criticism of the preliminary manuscript, to D. H. Sawin and J. C. Rhyne for their reviews of the final draft, to Julia Fahey for her careful copyediting, and to Marie Straniero for her excellent typing and editorial assistance. Finally, appreciation is extended to Burroughs Corp., Control Data Corp., Digital Scientific Corp., Hewlett Packard Company, Intel Corp., Interdata Inc., Microdata, Nanodata Corp., Standard Computer Corp., Varian Data Machines, and Western Digital Corp. for their reference materials, review of pertinent parts of the manuscript, and permission to reproduce appropriate illustrations.

The opinions expressed herein are those of the author and do not necessarily represent opinions of the U.S. Army or the Department of Defense.

Ft. Monmouth, New Jersey   Alan B. Salisbury

Chapter 1

Microprogramming in Perspective

1.1 INTRODUCTION

Microprogramming in one form or another has been part of the computer world for almost a quarter of a century! This may come as a surprise to those who view it as a relatively "new" field, especially when the short history of the entire computer industry is considered. The field of microprogramming has been evolving from the exclusive province of the computer designers into an area of potential utility to the much broader community of computer users and programmers. Thus, its recent elevation to a topic of general interest.

This first chapter briefly traces the evolution of microprogramming and introduces a number of related ideas and concepts. A major objective is to give the reader an understanding of the varying degrees to which a computer may be considered to be microprogrammable and the resulting impact this has on its generality. Additionally, some insight into current trends and possible future directions of the continuing evolutionary process may also be gained.

1.2 GENERALITY OF COMPUTERS

Computers have traditionally been classified into two categories, either *general purpose* or *special purpose,* terms that describe their applicability to problem solving. Rather than a discrete description of this nature, a continuous dimension including general purpose and special purpose machines at opposite ends could more accurately be used for such classification. In truth, some computers are more general purpose than others, and special purpose machines may vary

1

according to the number and variability of the tasks that they can perform.

Such a dimension is illustrated in Figure 1-1. At the extreme left we show the Universal Turing Machine, familiar to automata theorists, a totally programmable device with an absolute minimum of hardware—probably the most general purpose machine one could imagine. At the opposite extreme we show a fully hard-wired, non-programmable, special purpose computer capable of executing only a single task. The notion of *programmability* is key to this conceptual dimension, and it is manifested in a machine capability to accept externally supplied instructions that can cause it to perform a desired task. The more general purpose the machine, the more numerous and detailed instructions will be required to program it for a given task. There is thus an inverse relationship between hard-wired logic (hardware) and programmed instructions (software) running the length of the dimension.

While the above discussion is somewhat oversimplified and neglects a number of factors, nevertheless, it serves to illustrate the important concept of programmability and the interrelationship between hardware and software. The remainder of this discussion will be restricted to a much narrower range of the generality dimension (between dashed lines in Figure 1-1) into which fall the vast majority of today's commercially available and proposed computing systems.

1.3 THE CPU AND COMPUTER CONTROL

The central processing unit (CPU) of a digital computer can generally be subdivided into two basic functional segments, the first concerned with the transformation and movement of the data being processed and the second with the control of the CPU itself. This is illustrated schematically in Figure 1-2, in which the CPU is shown consisting of the arithmetic and logic element, and the control element. All movement and/or transformation of data is controlled primarily by signals emanating from the control unit which, in turn, behaves according to its internal logic and externally supplied "program." The program resides in main memory and is incrementally moved to the control unit in the form of "instructions." On the basis of the information contained in an instruction and the present status

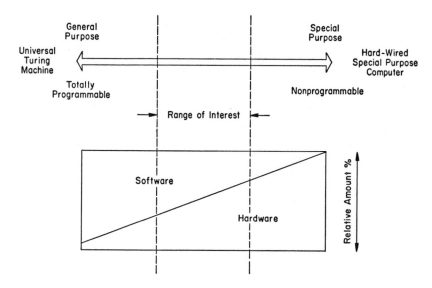

Fig. 1-1: Continuous Generality Dimension for the Description of Computer Applicability, Illustrating the Inverse Relationship Between Associated Hardware and Software.

of the machine, the control unit must thus issue control signals which: 1. specify what data movements and/or transformations (operations) are to take place; 2. specify which data (operands) are to be used; and 3. select and fetch the next instruction to be executed. These signals are ultimately applied directly as binary inputs to individual logic gates.

1.4 RANDOM LOGIC

In the so-called *hard-wired* computer, the control element is an assemblage of interconnected combinational and sequential logic networks that function as a *finite state machine*. The resulting pattern of gates and interconnections has become known as *random logic*, reflecting the ad hoc nature of the gate-by-gate (or chip-by-chip) design and resulting circuit board layouts.

Consider, for instance, a small computer with a single accumulator and, as part of the total instruction repertoire, several instructions that affect the accumulator contents. Among these instructions

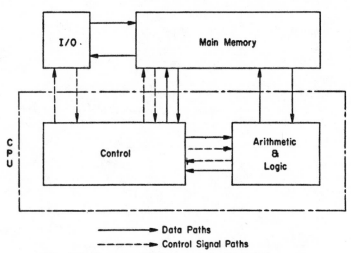

Data Paths
------- Control Signal Paths

Fig. 1-2: Functional Elements of a Digital Computer.

might be Clear and Add to the Accumulator (CLA), Add to the Accumulator (ADD), and Subtract from the Accumulator (SUB). Using the basic ADD capability, CLA can be accomplished by first clearing the accumulator and then performing the ADD; similarly, SUB can be accomplished by first complementing the number to be subtracted and then also performing the ADD. Assuming 16 clock pulses (CP0–CP15), are routinely provided for an instruction execution, they may be used to control the initiation of each of the tasks required for overall instruction execution.

In the interests of simplicity, it would probably be desirable to use the same numbered clock pulse to initiate the ADD function for each of the three instructions discussed. If CP10 were chosen for this purpose, it would then be possible to write a logic equation for the signal to be applied to the adder (for example, A) of the form:

$$A = (ADD + SUB + CLA) \cdot (CP10) \cdot (E)$$

This is interpreted as: Signal A is to be activated when the instruction register operation code is decoded as an ADD OR a SUB OR a CLA, AND clock pulse 10, execute phase, is also present. Similarly, if the signal that will cause the accumulator to be cleared is called C, and this is to occur at CP4 during the execution of the CLA instruction, we could have a (partial) logic equation:

$$C = (CLA) \cdot (CP4) \cdot (E)$$

Once again this is interpreted as: Signal C is to be activated when the instruction register operation code is decoded as CLA AND clock pulse CP4, execute phase, is present. Finally for this limited example, CP9 might be selected as the time to complement prior to adding for the execution of a SUB instruction. If N is the complementing signal we could have:

$$N = (SUB) \cdot (CP9) \cdot (E)$$

Next, consider that memory must be read both to fetch an instruction and to fetch operands. Perhaps instruction fetches are always performed at CP1 of the fetch cycle (F), and operands are always fetched at CP5 of the execute cycle for those instructions that require operands from memory (memory reference instructions = MR). Then the signal R, which is activated to initiate a memory read, might have for its equation:

$$R = (CP1) \cdot (F) + (MR) \cdot (CP5) \cdot (E)$$

The results of this very simplified portion of our design are shown in Figure 1-3. Each signal is developed on an ad hoc basis, taking into account the detailed conditions under which it is to be activated. Logic networks are developed for each one based on a simplified logic equation.

First, consider that only a few of the total number of functions actually required to implement the CLA, ADD, and SUB instructions were included in this analysis; second, note that only three related instructions were addressed. When this is expanded to all tasks required to implement an entire instruction repertoire, the reader can begin to appreciate the large number of logic equations involved and the varying sizes of the logic networks that may be required to implement them. This is the nature of the random logic design found in hard-wired computers.

1.5 THE MICROPROGRAMMED COMPUTER

In his classic paper of 1951, "The Best Way to Design an Automatic Calculating Machine,"[1] Maurice Wilkes sought to eliminate the

---

[1] See WILK51, bibliography.

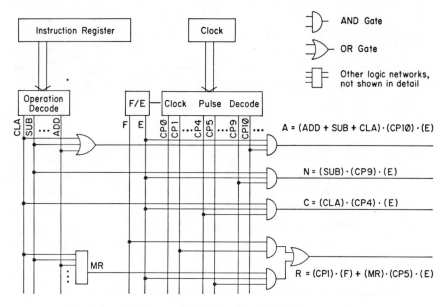

Fig. 1-3: An Elemental Portion of an Ad Hoc Random Logic
Control Unit Design.

randomness of control logic and replace it with an orderly logic matrix. As shown in Figure 1-4, Wilkes' scheme provided for the computer instruction (order) to be decoded to select a particular row of the matrix; the column elements of the selected matrix row would then be used on a one-for-one basis to issue the necessary control signals. A separate matrix contained the information required to select subsequent rows, based on the current row and possible conditional status information. Wilkes recognized that the execution of a machine instruction could logically be broken up into a sequence of elementary operations that he termed *micro-operations*. Each row of the combined matrix corresponded to a single microoperation and for the entire assemblage of microoperations he coined the term *micro-programme* from which we have the currently popular term *microprogram*.

The control matrices represent a form of memory in the computer. Each row can be considered as a single word in memory, with the connected (heavy dot) intersections indicating 1's, and the nonconnected intersections indicating 0's. A fixed control matrix thus is actually a *read-only* memory, as compared to the more conventional

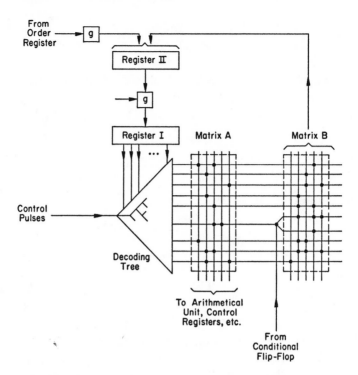

Fig. 1-4: Wilkes' Classical Design of a Micro-Control Unit.

read-write memory used for the main memory element of a typical computer.

One row of the control matrix (word of memory) can be thought of as a control instruction, or a microinstruction. *Microprogramming* can then be defined as the process of developing a set of microinstructions (control matrix contents) that execute from a separate control memory of a computer to govern the operation of the functional units of the computer.

With the availability of suitable electronic components for reasonably fast read-only memories (ROM's) in the mid 1960s, Wilkes' scheme was utilized with minor modifications in a number of commercial computers.[2] As Wilkes envisioned, microprogramming be-

---

[2] Predating most of the computers considered to be "microprogrammed," the Whirlwind I computer utilized many of the concepts; in particular, the WWI central control employed an orderly diode logic array not completely dissimilar

came a powerful tool of the computer designer. In addition to orderly simplicity, the principal advantages were that it allowed many design decisions to be postponed until the end of the design process and facilitated subsequent changes and modifications; the prime disadvantage was that available ROM technology yielded slower execution speeds than comparable hard-wired machines.

1.6 EVOLUTION THROUGH EMULATION

Wilkes subsequently speculated that it would be possible to "have a number of interchangeable matrices providing for different order codes, so that the user could choose the one most suited to his particular requirements."[3] This concept proved to be attractive as a solution to the "compatibility" problem. Microprogrammed computers of a new design could be equipped with additional read-only memories enabling them to *emulate* earlier computers and hence eliminating, at least for the moment, the necessity for reprogramming. This kind of compatibility has been referred to as *backward compatibility*.[4] Microprogrammed emulation has similarly enabled families of machines to be *upward* and *downward compatible* through a common basic machine language, even though the internal organizations and technologies employed have been very different from one model to another. Finally, *sideways compatibility* has similarly been achieved allowing one manufacturer's computers to emulate another.

While functionally similar to interpretation, *emulation*, for the purposes of this discussion, may be considered as the use of microprogramming techniques for the simulation of one machine by another. The machine doing the emulation is generally referred to as the *host machine* and the machine being emulated as the *target machine*. Occasionally, in the literature, the term *virtual machine* is used in lieu of target, and Wilkes has used *subject computer* and

---

from those of Wilkes. The operation control matrix could perhaps be considered one of the earliest "read-only memory" type controls. See SMIT59, bibliography.

[3] See WILK53, bibliography.

[4] Compatibility definitions are those of Husson. See HUSS71, bibliography.

object computer rather than host and target.[5] Host and target have become the predominant terms.

As an example of an upward/downward compatible family of computers, consider the IBM System 360 series. All models can be thought of as having a common architecture as seen by the programmer. In this sense, the 360 is a target machine and the different models are 360 emulators implemented on different host machines. Figure 1-5 illustrates this concept; the solid blocks are microprogrammed models, while the dashed blocks indicate the hard-wired models.[6] The varying range of performance characteristics of the host machines accounts for the resulting performance range of the different models of the 360 series.

1.7 THE MICROPROGRAMMABLE COMPUTER

Thus far, we have only considered microprogramming as a tool of the computer designer. Early microprogrammed machines were designed with the primary goal of implementing a particular architecture and instruction set; neither generality nor extendibility were major considerations. Modifications and emulation capabilities were accomplished through the design of new or modified read-only memories.

1.7.1 User Microprogramming

Microprogramming as a tool of the user has slowly evolved and is still greeted with less than enthusiasm (or active discouragement) by many manufacturers. Minicomputer manufacturers were probably the first to actively support user participation in the design process by making available facilities to assist in the design and checkout of ROM programs and by producing customized ROM's to meet special needs, primarily in the process control environment. Costs, lead-time,

---

[5] See WILK 69, bibliography.
[6] Philosophically, one can even think of the hard-wired models as being emulators. Further examination of emulation definitions and concepts can be found in SALI73.

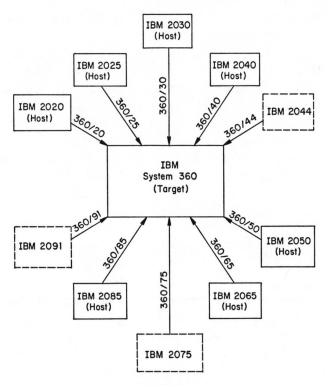

Fig. 1-5: IBM System 360
(Solid blocks indicate microprogrammed models).

and the relative difficulty of microprogramming combined to limit this mode of user participation.

1.7.2 Writable Control Store

The introduction of *writable control store,* control memory with a write as well as read capability, has given rise to what can truly be described as microprogramm*able* computers, in which not only the designer but the systems programmer and even the applications programmer can utilize the microprogramming capabilities to assist in problem solving The first microprogrammable machines included ROM for the bulk of the microprogram and a smaller amount of writable control store to enable the addition of new, special instructions to extend the basic repertoire or perhaps permit the microprogramming of special routines to speed up highly repetitive and time consuming tasks. Even in these machines, however, the microprogramming features primarily reflect the designer's intention of implementing a specified target machine; while it may be relatively easy to write microprograms to implement the intended machine, it may be commensurately difficult to write microprograms to accomplish different tasks.

Recently, machines have begun to appear that are fully microprogrammable (that is, they employ extensive if not exclusive writable control store) and whose architectures are intended to support general purpose microprogramming. With equal facility (difficulty) they may be microprogrammed to emulate a variety of different target machines or accomplish a variety of tasks. (Although this is the designer's intention, this capability is achieved with varying degrees of success.) The ultimate in machines of this type are those that have no machine language in the conventional sense, but are only microprogrammable; no specific higher level architecture was envisioned in their design.[7] Throughout this book, the term *microprogrammable* will be used to describe machines in which a significant portion of the control storage is writable or otherwise readily alterable.

1.7.3 The Universal Host

Several authors have discussed the designs of machines that can be considered to be *universal hosts,* that is, they can be microprogrammed to emulate any desired target machine.[8] Ideally, a universal host would be equally efficient in the emulation of all target machines; this is not an easy objective to achieve. The truly universal host must have a data structure and microinstruction repertoire that have in some way been optimized to accommodate emulation of the total range of target machine architectural parameters.

The notion of host machines being microprogrammed to emulate target machines is perhaps too restrictive, especially if the target machine is perceived as a machine language programmable computer. Indeed, a great deal of work has already been done in microprogram-

---

[7] See, for instance, OPLE67, ROSI71, and WILN72. Also see Chapters 6 and 7.
[8] See, for instance, ROSI69A, FLYN71A, and DAVP72, bibliography.

ming machines for the direct execution of higher level languages, microprogramming of operating systems, and even direct microprogramming of applications programs.

While not specifically considering microprogrammable machines, McKeeman made a strong argument for designing machines that would be "reasonably amenable hosts for the operating systems, compilers and popular languages presently in use" rather than merely to achieve an arbitrary architecture.[9] This philosophy can be extended even beyond applications to the concept of "environments" that are data oriented rather than program oriented.[10] Herein lie the goals of universality.

1.7.4. Dynamic Microprogramming

Just as conventional machines are multiprogrammed with pages swapped in and out of main memory, microprogrammable machines can be given the capability of swapping microprograms in and out of a writable control store, resulting in a form of *dynamic microprogramming*. With these same powerful multiprogramming techniques come many of the same problems, the principal one being protection (protecting programs from one another). This problem is somewhat compounded at the microprogramming level in that the microprogram is capable of altering the very structure of the machine. Solutions to this problem will probably take the form of microprogrammed operating systems (with perhaps some portions in read-only memory) including a system of modes and privileged microinstructions.[11]

There are those who question the user's need or desire to utilize microprogramming capabilities at all. They point out that today, generally, the user has available to him machine language programming capabilities that go unused in favor of higher level languages, operating system utilities, and the like. The answer to this challenge is twofold: First, there will always be users (although perhaps a

---

[9] See MCKE67, bibliography.

[10] The notion of environments is due to Rosin. See ROSI69A, bibliography..

[11] A description of an operating system designed to accommodate multiple emulators can be found in HOPK70.

relatively few) who can make the most of any capabilities provided to them; second, even if the applications user himself does not make direct use of microprogramming capabilities, the systems programmer can use them to great advantage when providing better compilers, run time environments, and such, which will benefit the user indirectly. A dynamic microprogramming capability can thus be of great benefit. In effect, it can provide a capability to dynamically "redesign" the architecture of the machine to meet the needs of the immediate job to be done.

1.8 FIRMWARE

A microprogram residing in a read-only memory has many of the attributes of conventional software; it is, as its name implies, a program. On the other hand, the applications programmer is normally able to write programs only in the higher level machine language of the system; to him the ROM and its microprogram are merely extensions of the hardware. In recognition of this dual status, the term *firmware* was coined to describe "microprograms resident in the computer's control memory [specializing] the logic design."[12]

It has been pointed out by Flynn and others that both hardware and software designers work with algorithms and that they differ only in the physical realization. Indeed, virtually any logic can be replaced with memory. If the memory is writable we can refer to its contents as software; if read-only, we can think of it as hardware. In either case, the term *firmware* can describe its functional utilization if not its complete implementation. Generally, however, manufacturers use the term *firmware* in conjunction with the read-only memory microprograms supplied with their processors.

1.9 MICROPROCESSORS AND MICROPROGRAMMING

An unfortunate similarity in terminology has resulted in a good deal of confusion concerning the subjects of microprocessors and microprogramming. The term *microprocessor* is generally used in

---

[12] See OPLE67, bibliography.

reference to a large-scale integrated circuit (LSI) processor on a single chip; with the addition of other LSI chips for memory, timing, and other auxiliary functions, a microprocessor may be expanded into a *microcomputer,* usually implemented on a single card or circuit board. The *micro* in microprocessor and microcomputer is thus a reference to the physical size of the units involved.

Use of the term *microprocessor* has also been made in the literature to describe a microprogrammed/microprogrammable processor. In this sense, *micro* refers to an architectural (logic) level below machine language instructions.

In order to make the distinction clear, all references to microprogrammed/microprogrammable processors and architectures within this book will use the terms *micro level processor* or *micro level architecture.* The term *microprocessor* will thus be restricted to mean an LSI processor on a chip. Microprogramming then does *not* equate to programming a microprocessor.

Having established this distinction, it can now be stated (with some trepidation) that some microprocessors are also microprogrammable and more have been microprogrammed in their logical implementation; in addition to being physically small in size, these microprocessors contain a micro level architecture to implement their instruction sets. Chapter 8 includes an example of such a processor.

1.10 ARCHITECTURE, ORGANIZATION, AND CONTROL

At least for the immediate future, we will continue to have a hierarchy of memory facilities available within a computer and its CPU. These will be referred to herein as *main memory, control store,* and *local store,* the latter consisting of the many functional registers of the CPU.

1.10.1 Levels of Control

Control store itself may have more than one level. In the hardwired machine, there is no control store. A microprogrammable machine contains a single level of control store. It is further possible that a micro level processor can itself be implemented utilizing a program in a second level of control store; the term *nanoprogrammable* has been coined to describe such a two-level control structure.[13] In theory, additional levels of control store can be added until the final hard-wired processor level is reached.

The highest level of control over the CPU is exercised by programs residing in main memory. *Macro-instructions* are referred to in most of the literature on emulation as equivalent to the conventional *machine instructions* found in main memory; such usage should not be confused with the more traditional connotation of macro's as being at a level above machine language instructions in many assembly languages. Within this book, the term *macro* will be used to refer to the machine language level, one level above micro. The lower level of a two-level control arrangement will be referred to as *nano*, in view of its rather well-established meaning.

1.10.2. Architecture and Organization Defined

Finally, it will be useful to differentiate between the terms *architecture* and *organization* as applied to computers. While they are used by some to mean different things, most use them virtually interchangeably. Within this book, *architecture* is reserved to refer to those aspects of a computer's structure that are visible to the programmer; this generally includes a set of registers, instruction formats, and an instruction repertoire. *Organization,* on the other hand, is at a level below architecture and is concerned with many items that are transparent to the programmer. In short, the term *architecture* is used to describe *what* facilities are provided, and the term *organization* to describe *how* those facilities are provided.

To illustrate this distinction, consider briefly the relatively common technique of fetching the next instruction in parallel with executing the current instruction, and assume that a branch is to take place. It is possible that in one machine the replacement of the prefetched instruction with the instruction that is being branched to will merely result in a delay of duration equal to a memory access time and the programmer will never be aware of it. It is also possible

---

[13] See NANO74, bibliography, and Chapter 7.

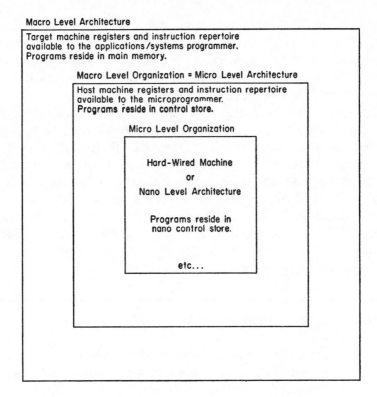

Fig. 1-6: An Illustration of the Hierarchical Structure
of Memories/Control Functions and the Differentiation
Between Architecture and Organization.

that in another machine the programmer must explicitly structure his instruction sequence to allow for this occurrence. In the former case we suppress the prefetch considerations to the organizational level; in the latter case, we elevate them to the architectural level. The concepts of levels of memory as related to the control function and architecture versus organization are illustrated graphically in Figure 1-6.

The focus of this book is on the architecture of microprogrammable machines. The following two chapters provide a comprehensive look at the many different architectural considerations associated with microprogrammable machines and define a set of descriptive parameters. These chapters are followed by a series of detailed case studies of representative, commercially available machines.

Chapter 2

Architectural Facilities
in Microprogrammable Machines

2.1 INTRODUCTION

In Chapter 1, computer architecture was defined to include those facilities of a machine that are visible to the programmer. Now we shall consider in some detail the architectural facilities of a microprogrammable machine.

The motivation for this study arises from an interest in machines with *general purpose*[1] microprogramming capabilities, and in machines said to be *universal hosts,* capable of emulating any target machine. These capabilities imply a high degree of generality in the machine architecture; therefore, we seek to describe and analyze the architectural parameters of microprogrammable machines with particular emphasis on those parameters that impact on generality.

The notion of generality should go beyond the mere ability to emulate a given set of target machines. It should also encompass the ability to support application environments directly in microprograms or, indirectly, through application oriented intermediate languages. Architectural facilities so oriented could be said to be *data directed* and are in consonance with McKeeman's concept of language directed computer design.[2] Unfortunately, little has been done about characterizing the architectural implications of different

---

[1] The term *general purpose* is used here to distinguish these machines from microprogrammed processors designed for the *special purpose* of implementing a particular machine language architecture and not intended for further microprogramming.

[2] The concept of *data directed* environments is due to Rosin. See ROSI69A, bibliography.

17

environments; on the other hand, target machines are tangible and their attributes are therefore more readily defined.

There is normally a trade-off between generality and efficiency. A micro level architecture designed to implement a single target machine will reflect the target design and require only a few (perhaps only one) microinstructions for the emulation of each machine instruction. When attempting to implement a highly dissimilar target machine on the same host, a large number of microinstructions would probably be required for each target machine instruction (if in fact exact emulation is feasible at all). Consider, for instance, the IBM 2050 processor on which the IBM System 360 Model 50 is implemented in microcode; one can readily envisage the difficulties that would arise in microprogramming this processor, oriented principally to 16- and 32-bit word lengths, to emulate the DEC PDP-10 computer with its 36-bit word length. Ideally, a universal host would require similar numbers of microinstructions per target instruction, regardless of the word lengths involved.

This chapter will first examine the primary characteristics of the hardware features of microprogrammable computers. The discussion here will concentrate on the data widths handled, the functional processing units available, and the local storage facilities that constitute the heart of the micro level architecture. The remainder of the chapter will consider control store, main memory, bus structures, interrupts, and input/output facilities.

2.2 DATA WIDTHS

The single most important factor impacting on the efficiency of emulation of a target machine by a given host is undoubtedly the data width(s) inherent in the host machine micro level architecture. When the host and target machine data widths do not match, the microprogrammer is faced with the task of creating a *virtual match* through the proper manipulation of the facilities available to him.

Two basic approaches have been taken in designing micro level architectures to handle this problem. The first approach is to provide a relatively wide data width with facilities for effectively reducing it to the desired number of bits. As an example, the MLP-900 (Standard Computer Corporation) provides a normal data width of 36 bits

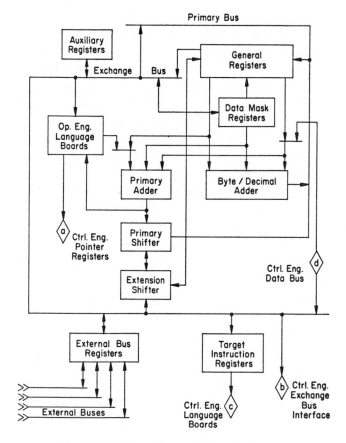

Fig. 2-1: MLP-900 Operating Engine Diagram
(Courtesy Standard Computer Corporation).

with a series of "data mask registers" that can be employed to mask out unwanted bits to achieve smaller widths. Figure 2-1 is a block diagram of the operating engine of the MLP-900. The data mask registers can be seen to affect the function of the general registers, the byte/decimal adder, and the primary adder.[3]

The second basic approach to handling different data widths is to provide a small data width that can be expanded into larger data

---

[3] The MLP-900 system includes an operating engine, a control engine, and control memory, plus optional auxiliary registers and main memory. See STAN70, bibliography.

widths, usually through iterative multiple precision micropro-gramming techniques. The Microdata MICRO 800 typifies this con-cept with an internal data width of 8 bits, as shown in Figure 2-2. Another example is the IBM 2020, host processor for the 360/20 system. The 2020 handles only a byte at a time, requiring several sequential actions to accommodate 360 halfwords (16 bits), full-words (32 bits), and double words (64 bits).

As an alternative to sequential microprogramming, physical con-catenation of modular units can be used to achieve wider data widths. The Burroughs Interpreter (basis for the commercial B700 line) uses this approach. Figure 2-3 shows a system with its modular building blocks. Each Interpreter Logic Unit processes 8 bits; effec-tive word widths of 8 to 64 bits can thus be achieved by coupling from one to eight logic units.[4]

Microprocessors (CPU's on a chip) may also employ both of these techniques. Iterative techniques are used with some (where timing is not critical), while many are designed to be physically coupled together to form larger units. The INTEL 3000 series, for instance, employs a basic 2-bit slice processor chip, providing great flexibility in realizable word widths.[5]

In the design of the B1700, Burroughs has combined the tech-niques of masking and iteration to achieve arbitrary data widths of from 1 bit to 65K bits. The nominal internal data width is 24 bits, and control facilities allow specification of the length of arithmetic operands to be operated on by the ALU. Fields of arbitrary length can be described in a field definition register, backed up by a bit addressable memory with no visible preferred word/byte bound-aries.[6]

2.3 FUNCTIONAL PROCESSING UNITS

The type, flexibility, accessibility, and number of functional units provided have a direct impact on both the generality and efficiency of a micro level architecture.

---

[4] See REIG72, bibliography.
[5] See Chapter 8 for a brief discussion of the INTEL 3000 series.
[6] The B1700 is fully described in Chapter 6.

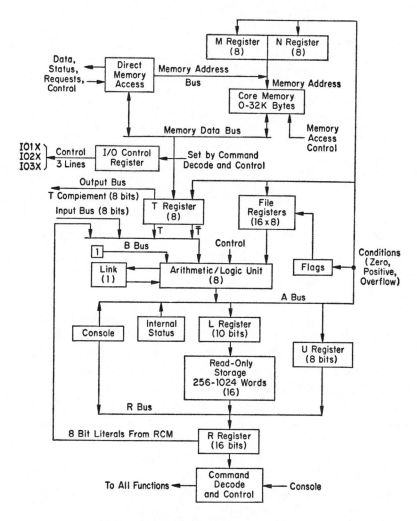

Fig. 2-2: MICRO 800 Block Diagram
(Courtesy Microdata Corporation).

Most common of the functional units is a conventional arithmetic and logic unit, or ALU. This generally provides basic functional operations including ADD, SUBTRACT, AND, OR, and so on, using full binary operands. Occasionally, multiplication and division capabilities are also included, but more often these are implemented by the microprogrammer.

Generality requires that the machine also be capable of processing

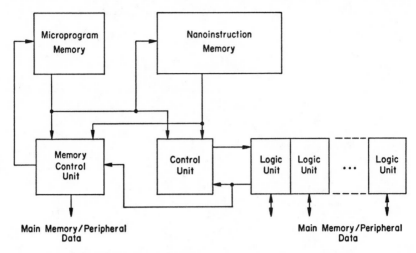

Fig. 2-3: Burroughs Interpreter System Block Diagram.

other arithmetic modes, as well as pure binary. These include decimal (4-bit binary) and, possibly, floating point; the latter varies in format considerably according to the particular target machine that is to be emulated. Figure 2-1 illustrates the provision of a separate adder for byte/decimal modes, while the primary adder handles the binary mode. The B1700 (Chapter 6) also provides a separate 4-bit ALU. The Interdata 8/32, on the other hand, employs a single ALU to handle multiple modes (including floating point); this is feasible since the 8/32 is designed to support a particular target machine architecture rather than as an attempt at a universal host.[7]

Shift capabilities may either be included in the ALU, or in a separate unit. A single-bit shift function is provided within the MICRO 800 ALU. The MLP-900 (Figure 2-1) employs a separate *primary shifter.* Similar units are called *skew* units, or *shift/rotate* units by other manufacturers. One of the most powerful of these separate shifting units is the barrel switch in the Logic Unit of the Burroughs Interpreter, shown in Figure 2-4; it is implemented as a matrix of gates that can shift a parallel input data word any number of positions left or right, logical or circular (end-around). Another alternative is to include shift/rotate capabilities in a multipurpose general register; this is the technique used by Burroughs in the B1700

---

[7]The Interdata 8/32 is fully described in Chapter 5.

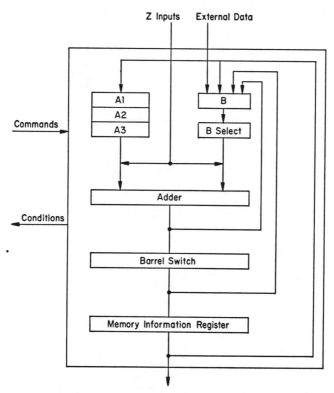

Fig. 2-4: Burroughs Interpreter Logic Unit.

(Chapter 6). The B1700 has several general registers that can be used to shift/rotate operands.

An important capability required for general purpose emulation, is the ability to *extract* a field of arbitrary length and position from a word or register. This is required to *decode* target machine instructions, operation codes, modifiers, register numbers, addresses, and so on, which are part of a target instruction and must be available for use by the microprogrammer in implementing an emulator.

Several techniques are used for providing extract capabilities. Without any special features, extraction can usually be accomplished through the use of several shift instructions (for an example, see Figure 2-5a). The B1700 has several registers that are addressable in 4-bit increments; these could be useful in extraction. It also has an explicit extract microinstruction that allows the microprogrammer to specify the right-most bit location and the field width to be ex-

a. Extraction by Shifting:

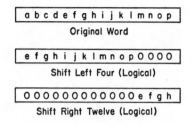

b. Extraction by Masking/Logical AND:

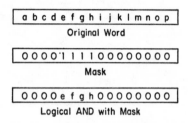

Fig. 2-5: Extraction of Bits efgh from a Register/Word.

tracted; this microinstruction operates on a special register designed to provide extract capabilities. Masking registers can be used in some cases for extraction, as can logical AND microinstructions (see Figure 2-5b). Finally, some machines provide special hardware assist features that must be tailored to specific target machine requirements. Figure 2-1 shows the MLP-900 target instruction registers feeding *language boards* that are built to specifications according to the target formats; such special hardware features do little for enhancing the actual generality of a machine.

Other hardware facilities may be dedicated to special functions also. An example is a special adder for the purpose of adding base and relative addresses in effective operand address calculations, as is found in the Interdata 8/32; once again, such a feature can be used only in emulating a particular target machine, or one very similar in architecture.

The flexibility of the functional units is critical to the generality of the micro level architecture, especially with regard to its emulation capabilities. Ideally, the ALU should be able to operate on operands of varying bit length and utilize various arithmetic conventions according to target machine requirements. Some bit length options were described earlier in the general discussion of data widths. Proper carry/borrow actions should occur for the operand length specified, and the capability for the microprogrammer to force carries/borrows out/in may assist multiple precision routines and arithmetic convention handling. The latter requires that the ALU should handle both 1's complement and 2's complement operands with equal facility. Finally, if separate ALU's are not provided to handle different modes (such as, binary, decimal, and so on), the primary ALU should have sufficient flexibility to handle multiple modes to support maximum generality. In practice, some machines come quite close to these ideals, with the most frequent departure in the handling of arithmetic modes.

Both accessibility and the number of units available impact greatly on efficiency through their more direct impact on concurrency of operations possible. *Concurrency* refers to the ability to perform operations in parallel, or simultaneously within the same execution cycle. A separate shifter, for example, generally permits both an arithmetic operation and a shift to be specified within the same microinstruction, as is the case with the MLP-900 and the Burroughs Interpreter. Contrast, for instance, the capabilities of the Interpreter's barrel shifter with the ALU single-bit position shift found in the MICRO 800; a three position shift in the former can be accomplished simultaneously with an addition, while in the latter machine three explicit shift microinstructions are required.

Accessibility is used to further describe whether or not the functional unit can be independently accessed, rather than being directly coupled to another functional unit. A completely independent shifter, for instance, could conceivably be shifting an operand altogether different from the results being generated by an adder.[8]

2.4 LOCAL STORAGE FACILITIES

Under local storage we include the various registers available to the microprogrammer. As with functional units, we are once again concerned with the type, number, and accessibility of these facilities.

---

[8] Such a capability could be exploited to create a "pipeline" architecture, taking maximum advantage of parallelism potentials.

Efficient emulation requires that the host machine have available to it at least as many dedicated and general purpose registers as the target machine being emulated. If a direct one-to-one mapping of target to host registers is not possible, the microprogrammer is forced to create a virtual match, probably using slower memory facilities to make up for insufficient host registers with a resulting loss of time and efficiency. A large number of general purpose registers thus increases the generality of the machine. A number of single-bit registers (flip-flops) usable for storing condition codes and other status bits may also be of great utility.

The Interdata 8/32 (Chapter 5) architecture permits up to eight *sets* of 16 general registers each; only one set is active at any given time and it is necessary to alter bits in the program status word (PSW) to change the set. In addition to a limited number of general registers, the B1700 (Chapter 6) includes a set of scratchpad registers to enhance local storage; these are not quite as powerful as general registers in that they can be accessed by only a few microinstructions, but they are faster and hence more efficient than memory locations for register mapping.

Special purpose registers frequently improve the efficiency of a machine. They may be either dedicated to a special function or may have a special capability in addition to a general purpose utility. The ability of several B1700 registers to shift/rotate, extract, and so on, has already been mentioned. Many machines designed as emulators have registers intended to support related target machine registers, such as a (macro) instruction counter and a (macro) instruction register; target instruction registers of the MLP-900 are an example.

Accessibility remains of paramount importance. Ideally, all local store facilities should be not only readable (testable), but writable (setable) as well. Since some of these registers are associated with control functions, writability implies great power and the inherent caution required of the microprogrammer. Readability may be either through direct or indirect addressing of the registers.

Indirect addressability of registers may be of particular utility in emulation. It can relieve the microprogrammer of the requirement to either decode a target machine register address, or move an address field from a target instruction into an implementing microinstruction field. This capability is used to advantage in the Interdata 8/32 (Chapter 5); a microinstruction may cite the YD register as a register address, rather than a specific general register, and the *contents* of the YD register will be used as the resulting specific register address.

Stacks of registers are of use for two reasons in particular.[9] First, they facilitate emulations of target machines that have stacks themselves. Second, they may be utilized to facilitate subroutines at the microprogram level. The B1700 (Chapter 6) includes a complete stack structure, while the Microdata 3200 (Chapter 4) includes a *stack head* (the first few elements of a stack, plus related support hardware) to facilitate implementation of a complete target (macro) level stack. Micro level subroutine facilities (such as a stack to hold return control store/microprogram addresses) enhance the general purpose nature of the architecture and improve potential efficiency by making it possible to eliminate redundant microprograms.

2.5 CONTROL STORAGE FACILITIES

The control storage architecture of a microprogrammable machine influences the generality of the machine. This section will briefly examine the functional characteristics, size, and structure of the control store. Additional considerations, related to the addressing of microinstructions, will be defined in Chapter 3.

Obviously it is desirable that most if not all of the control storage be read-write with comparable times for both functions. The necessity for this characteristic varies according to the operational environment. A good case can be made for designing a general purpose architecture that will be microprogrammed to function in a multitude of environments, but perhaps in only one environment for a given machine; in such a case a read-only memory is acceptable. A dynamic microprogramming environment, on the other hand, demands a full, high-speed read-write capability. Various technologies allow for intermediate characteristics employing *programmable*

---

[9] A *stack* or *pushdown stack* is a set of related registers that operate in a "last in—first out" manner. Each time an item is added to the stack, it becomes the top of the stack and the preceeding items are all pushed down one word; when the stack is accessed, the top of the stack can be removed and all remaining items pushed up. An analogy is a spring-loaded cafeteria tray storage facility.

ROM's or a facility to switch from one ROM to another. For some environments, such capabilities are adequate.

In addition to storage of microprograms, it may be desirable to utilize control store for implementation of target machine registers when insufficient general purpose micro level registers are available for this purpose. This implies a further requirement for control store to be read-write, at least in part; since control store is typically an order of magnitude faster than main memory, the efficiency of using control store for this purpose rather than main memory is apparent. It also implies the need for control store support registers independent from those associated with the microprogram as illustrated in Figure 2-6. Microprogram control is typically supported by a dedicated microprogram location counter register to hold the address of the next microinstruction to be accessed, and a microinstruction register to hold the current microinstruction. The control store address register and control store data register permit data to be written into or read from control store independent of the other two registers.

The size of the control storage may well limit the applications that can be successfully microprogrammed on a machine. It is therefore advantageous to facilitate reading programs from main memory into control store under microprogram control and writing from control store back to main memory. In concept, a virtual control store, similar to conventional virtual memory, would provide for the needed effective capacity; a microprogrammed basic operating system is probably the best way to achieve this goal. The B1700 (Chapter 6) permits microprograms to reside in main memory as well as control store.

Minimization and generality are essentially inconsistent when applied to control storage. It is possible to apply theoretical switching theory techniques to minimize entire control memories; since these techniques are totally dependent on the specific bit contents of the memory, they can only be employed to minimize a fixed microprogram and have no applicability to the general purpose microprogrammable machine. Subroutine facilities have already been mentioned as one means of reducing control storage size. The following chapter will discuss *residual control* and its capability to shorten microinstruction width, further reducing the overall size of a control store.

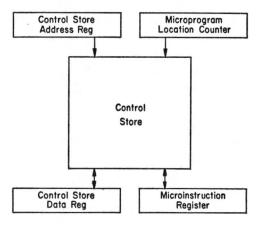

Fig. 2-6: Control Store and Associated Registers.

2.6 MAIN MEMORY

Just as target registers must be mapped to host facilities, so target main memory must be mapped to host memory. Thus, word width and the total number of words available are of interest when general purpose emulation is considered.

Techniques for handling variable data widths have previously been examined. The relatively slow access times of main memories make it highly desirable to have a wide memory data width to be reduced by masking or packing of words, rather than to rely on iterative accesses of smaller words to achieve wider effective widths.

Numbers of available words of main memory are usually limited by addressability. Generality requires that the addressing structure allow for the maximum practicable number of directly addressable locations, letting the microprogrammer do any required address mapping; this is in contrast to a limited number of directly address-able locations and use of secondary or auxiliary memory addressing to reach additional locations.

2.7 BUS STRUCTURES

Functional units, local store registers, control store, and main memory are interconnected to one another with a number of data paths usually referred to as *buses*. A bus is a parallel set of lines over which individual bits may be transferred, either in one direction (unidirectional) or two directions (bidirectional).

Bus structures are important in micro level architecture both with respect to the data width problem as described earlier and also for the flexibility they provide. A machine with only a few fixed buses will necessarily result in restrictions being placed on the microprogrammer. One alternative is to increase the number of buses and thus facilitate increased concurrency. Another alternative, as exemplified in the Nanodata QM-1 (Chapter 7), is to provide for a variable or switchable bus structure that can be set up and altered under microprogram control.

The number of major buses in a machine and the facilities connected to them may be reflected in the microinstruction structure and format. For instance, if an ALU has two buses providing inputs and the output is applied to a third bus, a three address microinstruction may be utilized; two addresses can specify *source* registers, and the third a *destination* register. This is the case with the Interdata 8/32. The MICRO 800 and MLP-900 (Figures 2-1 and 2-2) illustrate different bussing concepts and different address structures. Microinstruction formats will be discussed in more detail in the following chapter.

2.8 INTERRUPTS

Interrupt facilities are necessary for the micro level architecture itself and for many of the target machines to be emulated. For the sake of generality, interrupts should be *soft* rather than *hard;* that is, the interrupt itself should only set a bit for examination and subsequent handling by the microprogram rather than cause a predetermined control storage transfer. This permits the microprogrammer maximum flexibility both in timing and the method of handling emulated interrupts. Some hard interrupts may be required in practice to preclude catastrophic failure.

2.9 INPUT/OUTPUT

Requirements for input/output facilities depend on the environment in which the system is to be utilized and the objectives to be achieved. For general purpose microprogramming, including areas such as tailored instruction repertoire extensions, special function microroutines, and applications microprograms, the requirements are not usually overly demanding and any reasonably good I/O structure can probably provide the required support. In the particular case of emulation, however, the requirements may be very demanding and in many cases the I/O capabilities of the host processor become the limiting factor in the overall success of the emulator.

Just as it is necessary to create a mapping of target CPU facilities (such as local store registers) onto host CPU facilities, it is also necessary to create a similar mapping of target I/O devices to host I/O devices. The total set of functions performed from the invocation of a target I/O command to the final resulting action by the I/O device must then be provided for. This may include OS device handler actions, channel functions, controller functions, and finally the actions of the device itself. It is, of course, not essential that these individual functions be performed (emulated) on a one-to-one basis; the overall effect must, however, produce the desired end result.

Emulation of second generation target machines by microprogrammable processors is relatively easier than third generation target machines. I/O structures of second generation systems are comparatively simple, and the speed advantages of the microprogrammable processor generally overcome any other inefficiencies. Third generation target machines, on the other hand, may have sophisticated I/O structures, including an I/O *channel* that is essentially a small processor itself, dedicated to performing I/O functions. A single microprogrammable host processor will be hard pressed to efficiently perform the emulation of both the target CPU basic instruction set and the capabilities of an I/O channel as well. The best answer to this problem is probably the use of a separate processor to emulate I/O functions in detail; this is perhaps a good function to be considered for implementation using a microprogrammable microprocessor.

Chapter 3

Microinstructions and Control

3.1 INTRODUCTION

In Chapter 2, the major facilities available for use in a micro-programmable processor were discussed. This chapter now focuses on microinstructions as the mechanism through which the micro-programmer exercises control over these facilities, and then examines alternative control structures and techniques.

Generality exacts a price in terms of increasing the number of control signals required within the hardware. Each variable included to enhance the flexibility of a functional unit, for instance, must be specified before a microinstruction involving that functional unit can be executed. The result can be a commensurate increase in the complexity of the control structure of the microprogrammable processor. The impact of the added complexity of control of a processor varies according to the fundamental control structures and concepts utilized. One possibility is that microprograms can become much longer, consisting of many more low-level specialized microinstructions; another possibility is that individual microinstructions can themselves increase in complexity; still another approach is a combination of the two effects, with the added possibility that control information may not be entirely contained in a single microprogram, but may, in effect, be decentralized to multiple control substructures distributed in either space or time.

3.2 MICROINSTRUCTION FORMATS

A number of parameters may be used to describe microinstruction formats. In many cases these parameters are highly interrelated, but each conveys information of interest and significance. Generally, the commonly used parameters describe the length of microinstructions, the timing of their execution, the amount of control information and its degree of encoding, and the organization of information within the microinstruction.

3.2.1 Fixed/Variable Formats

Microinstruction formats can be categorized according to whether the format is fixed or variable. In the former case, each bit or field always has the same meaning, while in the latter, the same field may be utilized for different purposes and its function at any time is implicitly or explicitly specified by another field within the micro-instruction. Variable formats are more common and result in shorter microinstructions at the expense of additional logic to provide for the multiple function capabilities. As will be seen in the case studies, the QM-1 nano level architecture utilizes a fixed format structure, while the Interdata 8/32 and B1700 have variable formats. The Microdata 3200 format is relatively fixed, but the meanings of some fields may be conditioned by other fields.

3.2.2 Degree of Encoding

Even if a field is utilized for only a single purpose, the information within that field may be encoded to varying degrees. At one extreme, there may be no encoding at all, in which case each bit would directly connect to a control line (direct control); this implies that there would be one bit in the microinstruction for each control signal required within the hardware, which would require an extremely long or wide microinstruction. More typically, there is encoding of the control information to reduce the length, again at the expense of intermediate decode logic and time. The degree of encoding employed may be described as "little" or "highly" on a relative basis.

In addition to the requirement for additional logic, encoding may also impose a loss of flexibility. Unless all of the control signals grouped into a common field for encoding purposes are mutually exclusive, the fact that a single field output can activate only a single control signal at one time will restrict the amount of concurrency that can be provided for within a microinstruction; hence, great care must be taken in the establishment of such fields.

Consider as an example an ALU that can perform 16 arithmetic or logical functions, only one at a time. These 16 possible functions can be encoded into a 4-bit field with no loss of generality. Assume also that a separate shifter is available to manipulate the output of the ALU, and that a total of 16 shifting options (arithmetic, logical, and circular shifts) are available. Once again, the shift options may be encoded into a 4-bit field with no impact. The resulting ALU and shift control fields of a possible microinstruction are illustrated in Figure 3-1a. A total of 8 bits are required.

An alternative encoding scheme is shown in Figure 3-1b. Here a combined ALU/SHIFT control field is employed, and a single bit is used to "steer" the 4-bit control field to the appropriate decoder. This scheme requires only 5 bits in the microinstruction as opposed to the previous 8, which means every microinstruction (of this format) could be reduced in width by 3 bits. Now, however, only one operation can be activated by the microinstruction, either an ALU function *or* a shifter function.

If the ALU is indeed separate as stated above, then the hardware can probably perform the basic ALU operation and then shift the results in a single execution cycle and the two operations are not mutually exclusive. In this case, only the format encoding shown in Figure 3-1a is acceptable because it allows full concurrency. The format encoding of Figure 3-1b permits only one of the units to operate during the microinstruction execution cycle and hence precludes concurrency to save microinstruction bits.

On the other hand, if the ALU/shifter were in fact an integral unit physically capable of performing one of the 32 possible ALU/shift operations during a cycle, then the format encoding of Figure 3-1b would be the appropriate one, and Figure 3-1a would represent a waste of control word bits. These examples serve to illustrate the concept of encoding of mutually exclusive control functions into a common field.

Before leaving the subject of encoding, some timing/speed considerations should be mentioned. Any encoding normally implies a subsequent requirement for decoding. Decode logic, like any other logic, takes a finite time from application of inputs to the activation of the corresponding outputs. Even the encoding of mutually exclusive bits results in a penalty of added execution time. The use of one field to steer or otherwise condition the meaning of another (encoded) field, in effect, adds another level of encoding and may result

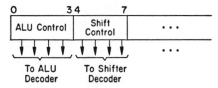

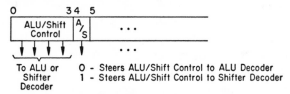

Fig. 3-1: Impact of Encoding Techniques on Concurrence.

in a further accumulative delay time. This is a good example of classical time/(bit storage) space trade-offs.

3.2.3 Number of Control Fields

In order to maintain maximum flexibility and consequently provide for the most powerful microinstructions consistent with hardware capabilities, there should be a separate field within the microinstruction for each independently controllable functional unit or facility. This will permit all possible simultaneous operations to be specified. A high degree of possible concurrency places a considerable burden on the microprogrammer to take full advantage of possible parallel operations. In fact, not all allowable concurrent actions may be useful from a practical point of view.

The number of control fields can also be expanded by including multiple fields that can be applied to the same control signals at different times. This concept is discussed further in the following section.

3.2.4 Microinstruction Timing

The basic timing consideration of microinstructions is the number of clock cycles during which the microinstruction remains effective.

Monophase[1] or *single-phase*[2] machines are those in which the micro-instruction is in effect for only a single clock pulse (or cycle). More specifically, all control signals are generated by the microinstruction simultaneously. If, on the other hand, for a single microinstruction control signals are issued in sequence over a number of clock pulses (cycles) the machine can be described as being *polyphase* or *multiple-phase*.

Generally, a multiple-phase system has a fixed timing structure. It is possible, however, to include within the microinstruction explicit information about the time phasing of the control signals to be used. Alternatively, operation codes may implicitly determine the timing.

The QM-1 is one example of a machine with variable time phasing; a single nanoinstruction bit can be set to cause the execution cycle to be stretched to double the normal execution time. In addition, the QM-1 also has multiple sets of control fields within a nanoinstruction that are activated sequentially.

3.2.5 Horizontal/Vertical Microinstructions

The most common classification applied to microinstructions is to describe them as *horizontal* or *vertical* in format type. The discussion of this parameter has been delayed until now because it cuts across many, if not all, of the preceeding descriptors. Further, there are no universal definitions of the terms and the literature contains many somewhat different uses of them.

Microinstruction word length by itself is not sufficient to determine whether a machine should be classed as horizontal or vertical, since several previously mentioned factors directly affect bit length. Nevertheless, *short word* and *long word* microinstruction types have been used to characterize machines;[3] short word and vertical have often been equated, as have long word and horizontal.

Timing has been considered by some to affect the horizontal/vertical classification decision. Gschwind's definition of vertical is essentially equivalent to what was described earlier as single-phase or

---

[1] Monophase/polyphase terms are described in REDF71.
[2] Single/multiple-phase terms are described in RAMA72.
[3] See, for instance, BELL72, and ROSI71, bibliography.

monophase and his definition of horizontal is similarly equivalent to multiple-phase/polyphase;[4] the latter terms better fit his descriptions.

Ramamoorthy and Tsuchiya draw their distinction solely on the basis of the number of control fields (operation codes) present: A single field indicates a vertical microinstruction and multiple fields indicate horizontal microinstructions. This is an appropriate description only if it is restricted to single-phase microinstructions. The point here is that several short word type instruction fields can be combined into a single microinstruction for efficient control memory accessing and then executed sequentially in a like number of clock cycles. This, in principle, should still be considered vertical microprogramming. In their earlier paper, Ramamoorthy and Tsuchiya describe the two types of formats as *function/field type* (horizontal) and *machine code type* (vertical).[5]

A more meaningful distinction between the two lies in the relative capability to exercise detailed (and nearly direct) control over the hardware. This capability is achieved to a far greater degree in the horizontal machine, and one consequence is normally a wider microinstruction. Many separate control fields are required for all of the controllable facilities with minimum resultant encoding and generally a fixed rather than a variable format. Redfield has aptly chosen to additionally describe this as *hard microprogramming* due to its close association with the hardware.[6] It meets Flynn's criterion that all separate functional units are controllable during a single execution as well as Rosin's view that individual bits select specific data paths in such control word type microinstructions.[7]

Machines with greater parallel processing capabilities tend to be more horizontal than vertical, although one does not necessarily imply the other. Independent functional units are best served by separate control fields in the microinstruction, and, as previously mentioned, a lesser degree of encoding assures no loss of possible flexibility in simultaneous control signal capabilities. These two factors combine to create longer microinstruction words with more

---

[4] See GSCH67, bibliography.
[5] See RAMA69; RAMA70, bibliography.
[6] See REDF71, bibliography.
[7] See FLYN71A, ROSI69A, bibliography.

direct control over the hardware for machines with significant parallelism.

In summary, then, a preferred definition of *horizontal microprogramming* would include a requirement for a sufficient number of separate control fields to exercise simultaneous control over all independent hardware facilities, with encoding limited to mutually exclusive control signals. *Vertical microprogramming,* on the other hand, is further removed from the hardware (hence it could also be called *soft microprogramming*), employs variable formats, a high degree of encoding, and, in many ways, resembles conventional machine language programming. Vertical microinstructions are not as powerful as are horizontal in that much of the flexibility (that is, simultaneous control signal combination possibilities) is necessarily lost. A typical vertical microinstruction has a single operation code (with or without modifiers) and one or more address field, while horizontal microinstructions may well have no address part at all since the control signals are directly applied to registers, data paths, and functional units.

Figure 3-2 illustrates examples close to the two extremes. The horizontal example in Figure 3-2a is the microinstruction for the IBM 2050 processor used to emulate the IBM System 360 Model 50; it contains over 25 separate fields in its 90-bit microinstruction, controlling independently an adder, mover, shifter, and address generation logic. By contrast, the Microdata 800 vertical example contains only 16 bits with a single operation code field and modifiers.

The parameters used to describe microinstructions are summarized in Figure 3-3, along with their typical association with the horizontal/vertical classification. While the definitions (descriptions) presented herein are by no means universally accepted, they nevertheless capture the essence of the critical issues involved. The last element in the figure, microinstruction sequencing, has yet to be discussed and is the subject of the following section.

3.3 MICROINSTRUCTION SEQUENCING

There are two aspects of microinstruction sequencing techniques to be examined. The first of these concerns the timing of microinstruction fetches and the second concerns address generation.

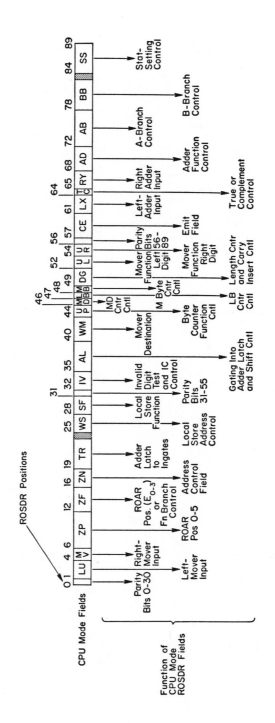

Fig. 3-2a: A Horizontal Type Microinstruction (IBM 2050).

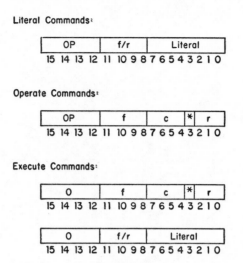

Fig. 3-2b: A Vertical Type Microinstruction (Microdata 800).

3.3.1 Fetch Timing

We will touch only briefly on the timing of fetches of microinstruction since more often than not this is an organizational rather than architectural consideration. The terms *serial* and *parallel* can be used to describe when fetches take place. In a serial case the next microinstruction is not fetched until the current microinstruction has completed its execution (see Figure 3-4a). All necessary information is thus available to determine the correct microinstruction to be fetched next. The parallel system, on the other hand, provides for the next microinstruction to be fetched concurrent with the execution of the current microinstruction, with its obvious speed advantages (Figure 3-4b). Conditional branches may create a problem in the parallel case since all required information for the determination of the next address may not be available until the completion of the execution of the current microinstruction. Frequently, the system will make a "best guess" as to what the actual next address will be. If the guess is correct, no time is lost; if incorrect, at least a fetch cycle will be lost (Figure 3-4c). It is possible that the microprogrammer may be required to participate in the best guess or fix-up determination and, in that case, he should have an understanding of the overlap techniques involved.

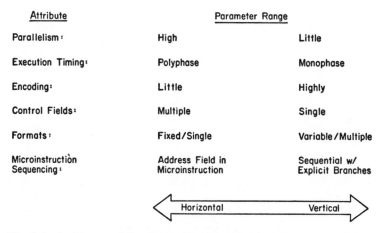

Attribute	Parameter Range	
Parallelism:	High	Little
Execution Timing:	Polyphase	Monophase
Encoding:	Little	Highly
Control Fields:	Multiple	Single
Formats:	Fixed/Single	Variable/Multiple
Microinstruction Sequencing:	Address Field in Microinstruction	Sequential w/ Explicit Branches

Horizontal ← → Vertical

Fig. 3-3: Architectural Parameter Ranges and their Typical Association with Horizontal/Vertical Classification.

3.3.2 Next Address Selection

A great many techniques have been employed for microinstruction address generation in microprogrammable machines. Under close examination they can be grouped into a relatively few general techniques with specific implementations using minor variations.

The original Wilkes technique was adequate for microprogrammed machines but is inadequate for microprogrammable machines owing to its physical alteration of the address portion of the matrix when conditional branch microinstructions are involved. Nevertheless, the basic technique of including the address of the next microinstruction within the current microinstruction is frequently utilized (with a different technique from that of Wilkes for handling conditional branches). A second basic technique for other than conditional branch microinstructions is to provide an incrementing capability on the microinstruction address register and execute from sequential locations in control store. In this scheme it is necessary to include an unconditional branch capability not required in the modified Wilkes scheme since in the latter case every microinstruction that is not a conditional branch is effectively an unconditional branch.

A microprogrammable machine requires that all of control store be uniformaly structured so that different microprograms can be loaded at different times. For this reason the Wilkes scheme for

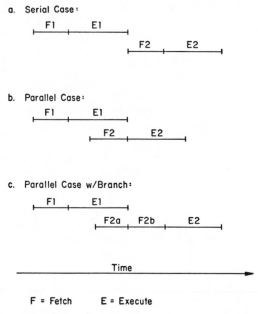

a. Serial Case:

b. Parallel Case:

c. Parallel Case w/Branch:

Time

F = Fetch   E = Execute

Fig. 3-4: Microinstruction Fetch Timing Considerations.

handling of conditional branches must be modified. When a micro-instruction includes the address of its successor, it is common to include a field in the microinstruction that can specify one or more tests to be applied before the next address is finally determined. The IBM 360/50 microinstruction, for example, includes a base (high-order) address and several test fields for determining the low-order bits according to available status information (see fields ZP, ZF, AB, and BB, Figure 3-2a). With all possible successor microinstructions stored in consecutive locations, the low-order bits are sufficient to determine which one should be selected. Alternatively, a microinstruction format may explicitly include more than one successor address in every microinstruction, with one or more test fields used to make the selection. In such a case two possible alternatives is a reasonable limit, with cascaded branch instructions used for other than two-way branches.

Normally, incrementing schemes must also make special provisions for conditional branches. Many vertical machines utilize schemes very similar to conventional machine language programming for conditional branches, with two-way branch-on-condition or skip-on-condition opcodes. Test masks may also be specified to provide for replacement of the sequentially generated address by a new address selected from one or more other registers whose contents may be gated to the microinstruction address register. An example of the latter techniques is the Honeywell H4200, which permits selection from up to five possible alternative addresses.[8]

In summary, two basic techniques for next address selection have been considered, an explicit address field in every microinstruction or an incrementing microinstruction address register. The following general techniques for handling conditional branches have also been considered: multiple address fields within microinstructions; constructive address generation (high-low/low-order bit selection); address replacement from external registers; and more conventional test/branch or test/skip instructions. Other schemes can, of course, be described, but generally they will be found to be related to. the above.

Most vertically microprogrammed machines employ the sequential scheme that is most efficient when a high degree of *locality* or *proximity* (consecutive microinstructions are physically stored in sequence) is present in the microprograms. Horizontal systems that can interpret macro-instructions with as few as one microinstruction more effectively apply the modified Wilkes technique of explicit address fields due to the high incidence of unconditional branches encountered.

3.4 MICROINSTRUCTION REPERTOIRE

As much as any other area, the impact of the microinstruction repertoire on the generality of a micro level architecture requires a good deal of additional research. Even at the macro level there has not been adequate research to determine what indeed is an optimum instruction repertoire. Typically, machine design has been more "bottom up" than "top down" in nature. The notion of generality of the repertoire has been at best a qualitative one and rarely a quantitative one. At the macro level we are beginning to see concern with *primitives,* operations oriented to particular application areas that are basic to that application and can greatly facilitate its implementation

---

[8] A full description of the H4200 can be found in HUSS71, bibliography.

if available as machine instructions. Similar information must be available if an optimal microinstruction repertoire is to be determined.

In the absence of knowledge of what in fact constitutes an optimum set of primitives, the horizontal or hard machine architecture is certainly more general. In effect, the fully horizontal machine has either "no" repertoire or an "unlimited" repertoire since the total capabilities of the machine are accessible by the microprogrammer. Vertical machines, on the other hand, have compromised between alternative combinations and have inherently less generality.

As a minimum, of course, the microinstruction repertoire should provide access to all of the capabilities of each functional unit. This causes a proliferation in the number of opcodes in the vertical machine and the number of bits per microinstruction in the horizontal machine. This is in part the bottom up approach alluded to earlier. The top down approach provides for the inclusion of microinstructions oriented to tasks to be accomplished in the many environments the machine is to support. As an example, microinstructions that can facilitate table look-up operations will be extremely useful in compilation; microinstructions that can handle queue operations will similarly assist operating system coding.

A trade-off normally exists between power and generality. The more powerful a microinstruction, the more limited its applicability to different environments. If macro-primitives were known for most application environments, it would then be possible to determine a set of microprimitives to support them, and hence restrict the power of microinstructions to that which is consistent with the desired generality.

There are many who fear that powerful microinstructions are dangerous tools when provided to the user microprogrammer. Power in this sense generally refers to the ability to communicate on a nearly direct basis with the hardware rather than through the usual protection offered by an operating system. One solution to the potential problems that arise here is to provide for privileged microinstructions or modes that can only be entered by activating certain control features (such as a console switch). We have already discussed the implementation of a basic operating system that would reside in control memory and that could similarly control access to privileged microinstructions.

3.5 MICROPROGRAMMING LANGUAGES

Since this book is about computer architectures, the overwhelming emphasis is properly on hardware; nonetheless, a few words on software considerations are in order at this point.

Unlike macro level machines that are heavily supported with manufacturer supplied compilers for the most popular languages (FORTRAN, BASIC, ALGOL, PL/1, COBOL), microprogrammable machines generally do not have translators from higher order languages to microcode readily available. Indeed, in some cases where the manufacturer still resists user microprogramming, no support software is provided at all.

The most commonly provided software support package is an assembler that translates symbolic instructions on a one-to-one basis into executable microinstructions. These are backed up occasionally by debug packages to aid the microprogrammer in finding and fixing problems in his microprogram.

Assemblers for vertically programmed machines are commonplace and differ very little from assemblers typically provided for machine language level application. Horizontal machines, on the other hand, pose a more difficult problem. The simple translation of symbolic/mnemonic data into necessary binary codes is comparatively straightforward; the difficulty lies in assisting the microprogrammer to make effective use of the horizontal machine's possibilities for concurrency without burdening the microprogrammer with all the inherent problem areas and limitations. Available assemblers for horizontal machines have achieved limited success from this standpoint. Much work remains to be done in this fertile field.[9]

3.6 CONTROL STRUCTURES

The control concepts employed within a machine affect the complexity of the microprogramming task and also the requirements for microprogram storage. The following sections address distribution of control information, the frequency of its change, and levels of

---

[9] For a good discussion of microprogramming language, see AGRA74.

control. Some novel architectures illustrating some of the concepts are also introduced.

3.6.1 Distributed and Centralized Control

Most microprogrammable processors employ what can be termed *centralized control,* in which all control is governed by a single monolithic control unit; the entire microprogram in such a case resides in a central control store. At the opposite extreme there might be many independently controllable units, each with its own store of control information. Rather than a single centralized microprogram, there would, in effect, be many individual microprograms that collectively control the functions of the entire processor through what can be described as *distributed control.* Many processors in practice lie somewhere in between the "pure" centralized control concept and a fully decentralized concept.

At the system level, a multiprocessor system could be considered as an example of a system with distributed control. Each processor contains its own program and can perform its own tasks with only occasional direction received from a master processor. Microprogrammable processors may similarly be organized into a larger system, while each retains its own microprogram to control its particular functions. Burroughs Interpreters are frequently utilized in such a manner.

It is also possible to employ distributed control *within* a processor. In such a case, functional units retain a certain amount of local control and require less control from the central control unit. Many processors exhibit this characteristic to some degree, if only by having decode logic local to each functional unit, or using special control registers associated with the functional units; in either case, the externally supplied control information required by these functional units is reduced.

A more interesting concept of distributed control is one in which individual functional units can actually be microprogrammed to perform different tasks within a processor, and perhaps their interconnection within the processor can be altered. Such a scheme could be employed to create a variable structured *pipelined* machine in which consecutive functional units perform different processing or transformation functions on data in assembly line fashion.[10]

An example of an architecture based on distributed control is Lesser's Dynamic Control Structure shown in Figure 3-5. He specifies two different internal languages for its control: A Structure Building Language is used to define the control structure of each process including input and output data sets and activation sequences, and an Integer Function Language is used for general arithmetic and logical computation such as in the simulation of functional units. The architecture is designed specifically for emulation, and its capability of tailoring the hardware into a virtual machine reflecting the architecture of the target machine adds greatly to its effectiveness.[11]

Levy's Z-Machine (Figure 3-6) is another example of multiple microprocessors that can work in a master-slave mode to jointly perform computational tasks. Unlike Lesser's architecture, however, Levy's is essentially a fixed structure. All of the Z-Machine processors have access to a common microprogram store, but can function independently. Therefore, it exhibits both distributed and centralized control characteristics. The allocator shown in the figure determines the assignment of slave processors and maintains detailed status information on all processors.[12]

3.6.2 Residual Control

On examination, control information may be loosely classified as relatively "dynamic" or "static," according to the frequency with which it is altered. During any given emulation a significant amount of otherwise variable information (such as data word width, arithmetic conventions, and so on) can probably be specified at the beginning of the emulation and thereafter remain unchanged. Special purpose registers in the local store can be utilized to hold this

---

[10] The advantages of a microprogrammable pipeline have been described in BARS71. Also, a discussion of the timing and interactive control problems inherent in distributed control, with particular emphasis on two and three control element CPU's, can be found in MCCL71. See bibliography.

[11] For additional details, see LESS71, LESS72, bibliography.

[12] See LEVY73, bibliography.

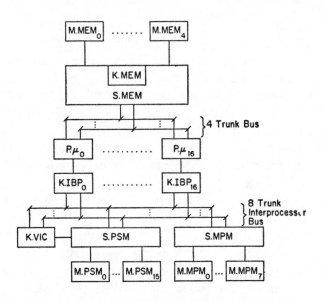

M.MEM$_i$ — main memory module i, where M.MEM is interleaved on
low order bits four ways, cycle time of 2 μsec.

S.MEM — 4 by 4 crosspoint switch for access to modules of
main memory.

K.MEM — control used for aligning bit string.

P.μ_j — one of 16 microprocessors, cycle time of 1 μsec.

K.IBP$_j$ — control used for scanning 8 trunk interprocessor bus.

K.VIC — virtual interaction controller.

S.PSM — 8 x 16 crosspoint switch for access to modules of
process space memory.

M.PSM$_i$ — process space memory module i, where M.PSM is
interleaved 16 ways, cycle time of 2 μsec.

S.MPM — 8 x 8 crosspoint switch for access to modules of
microprogram memory.

M.MPM$_i$ — microprogram memory module i, where M.MPM is
interleaved eight ways, cycle time of 2 μsec.

Fig. 3-5: Lesser's Dynamic Control Structure
Architecture for Emulation.

information. Such registers, commonly referred to as *stats* or *set-up*
registers, provide a form of *residual control* and reduce the control
problem to the specifications of the more dynamic information;
residual control can thus permit a reduction in microinstruction
word length.[13] Essentially, it can be considered a special form of
distributed control.

---

[13] See, for instance, DAVP72, FLYN71A, bibliography.

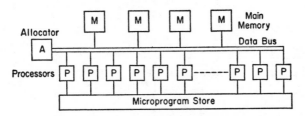

Fig. 3-6: The Z-Machine Architecture.

One machine employing a form of residual control is the Nanodata QM-1 (fully described in Chapter 7). The QM-1 has F store registers, for instance, that are used to specify bus connections between functional units and local store registers. Additionally, the F store exercises limited control over the arithmetic mode of the ALU.

3.6.3 Multilevel Control

In 1962, Grasselli described a two-level control store scheme of novel design.[14] At the lowest level he envisioned a read-only memory with microinstructions (presumably long word horizontal type) arranged in random order, with each one appearing only once. The upper level of control memory would contain "information about the microprogram," and in essence would simply contain addresses to cause a particular sequence of lower level microinstructions to be executed.

One of the first machines with a true two-level control store is Nanodata's QM-1. While not utilizing Grasselli's concept exactly, the QM-1 does have long word horizontal type nanoinstructions at the lower level and permits short word vertical type microinstructions at the upper level. Just as a microprogrammable machine allows the microprogrammer to define a target machine's macro level architecture, so does a nanoprogrammable machine allow the nanoprogrammer to define a target micro level architecture.[15]

Closer to the Grasselli concept is the Burroughs Interpreter, although it too has its differences. The Interpreter utilizes a *split* memory for control store, divided into a *microprogram memory* and

---

[14] See GRAS62, bibliography.
[15] Alternatively, these two levels have been described as "mini" and "micro" in RAMA72, bibliography.

MICRO CONTROLS

1	2	3	4	5	6	7	8	9	10	11	12	13	14	15	16
0	∅	*	SAR					∅	∅	∅	∅	∅	∅	∅	∅
1	0	*	SAR					LIT							
1	1	0	∅	*	AMPCR										
1	1	1	0	∅	∅	∅	∅	LIT							
1	1	1	1	*	NANO ADDRESS										

∅ Unused
* Shorter fields are right justified

NANO CONTROLS

Parentheses surround optional lexic units, provided by default.

Brackets contain DC 2000 mnemonics

? Codes not produced by TRANSLANG.

8	9	10	Condition Adjust -- CAJ
0	0	0	--
0	0	1	SET LC2
0	1	0	SET GC2
0	1	1	RESET GC
1	0	0	SET INT
1	0	1	SET LC3
1	1	0	SET GC1
1	1	1	SET LC1

1	2	3	4	Condition Tested Result is Boolean cnd
0	0	0	0	GC1
0	0	0	1	GC2
0	0	1	0	LC1
0	0	1	1	LC2
0	1	0	0	MST
0	1	0	1	LST
0	1	1	0	ABT
0	1	1	1	AOV
1	0	0	0	COV
1	0	0	1	SAI [RMI]
1	0	1	0	RDC
1	0	1	1	LC3 [RMA]
1	1	0	0	EX1 [EXT]
1	1	0	1	INT
1	1	1	0	EX2 [SRQ]
1	1	1	1	EX3 [URQ]

11	12	13	Successor			14	15	16

			Then Part Used if SC=1 to MPAD Ctls		Else Part Used if SC=0		
0	0	0	WAIT	0	0	0	
0	0	1	(STEP)	0	0	1	
0	1	0	SAVE	0	1	0	
0	1	1	SKIP	0	1	1	
1	0	0	JUMP	1	0	0	
1	0	1	EXEC	1	0	1	
1	1	0	CALL	1	1	0	
1	1	1	RETN	1	1	1	

5	FT Condition Value
0	NOT $\overline{cnd}$=:SC
1	-- cnd=:SC

6	Logic Unit Conditional
0	Do Unconditionally
1	Do Conditionally if SC

7	Ext Op (MDOP/CAJ) Conditional
0	Do Unconditionally
1	Do Conditionally if SC

17	18	19	Adder X Input
0	0	0	(0)
0	0	1	LIT
0	1	0	ZEXT [EXT]
0	1	1	CTR
1	0	0	Z
1	0	1	A1
1	1	0	A2
1	1	1	A3

20	21	22	23	24	25	26	Adder Y Input
0	0	-	-	-	-	-	B0--
0	1	-	-	-	-	-	BT--
1	0	-	-	-	-	-	BF--
1	1	-	-	-	-	-	B1--
-	-	0	0	0	-	-	B-0-
-	-	1	0	0	-	-	B-T-
-	-	-	-	-	0	0	B--0
-	-	-	-	-	0	1	B--T
-	-	-	-	-	1	0	B--F
-	-	-	-	-	1	1	B--1
Comp	1	0	0	Comp			B-F-*
Comp	0	0	0	Comp			B-1-*
0	0	0	0	1	0	1	LIT
0	0	0	1	0	0	0	ZEXT [EXT]
0	1	0	1	1	0	0	CTR
0	1	1	0	1	0	1	Z
0	0	1	1	0	0	1	AMPCR [L0]
0	1	1	1	1	0	1	Others ?

*Use Adder Operation with Complement Y

Fig. 3-7: Interpreter Microprogram Reference Card
(Courtesy Burroughs Corporation).

INTERPRETER
MICROPROGRAMMING REFERENCE CARD

27		Inhibit Carries into Bytes
0	--	Allow
1	IC	Inhibit

28	29	30	31		Adder Operation		
							Logic
0	0	0	0	X	+	Y	
0	0	0	1	X	NOR	Y	$\overline{X}\ \overline{Y}$
0	0	1	0	X	NRI	Y	$\overline{X}\ Y$
0	0	1	1	X +	Y +	1	
0	1	0	0	X	NAN	Y	$\overline{X} \vee \overline{Y}$
0	1	0	1	X	OAD	Y	$X + (X \vee Y)$
0	1	1	0	X	XOR	Y	$X\ \overline{Y} \vee \overline{X}\ Y$
0	1	1	1	X	NIM	Y	$X\ \overline{Y}$
1	0	0	0	X	IMP	Y	$\overline{X} \vee Y$
1	0	0	1	X	EQV	Y	$X\ Y \vee \overline{X}\ \overline{Y}$
1	0	1	0	X	AAD	Y	$X + (XY)$
1	0	1	1	X	AND	Y	$X\ Y$
1	1	0	0	X -	Y -	1	$X + \overline{Y}$
1	1	0	1	X	RIM	Y	$X \vee \overline{Y}$
1	1	1	0	X	OR	Y	$X \vee Y$
1	1	1	1	X	-	Y	$X + \overline{Y} + 1$

32	33		Shift Type Selection for BSW
0	0	--	No Shift
0	1	R	Right End Off
1	0	L	Left End Off
1	1	C	Right Circular

34	35	36		A Register Input from BSW
0	0	0	--	No Change
1	-	-	A1	
-	1	-	A2	
-	-	1	A3	

37	38	39	40		B Register Input Select
0	0	0	0	--	No Change
0	0	0	1	BC4	Comp 4 Bit Carries
1	0	0	0	BAD	Adder
1	0	0	1	BC8	Comp 8 Bit Carries
1	0	1	0	BBA	BSW v Adder
1	0	1	1	B	BSW
1	1	0	0	BEX	External
1	1	0	1	BMI	MIR
1	1	1	0	BBE	BSW v External
1	1	1	1	BBI	BSW v MIR
	Others			?	

41		MIR Input from BSW
0	--	No Change
1	MIR	

42		AMPCR Input from BSW
0	--	No Change
1	AMPCR	

43	44	45	46		Mem Dev Address Input	
0	0	0	-	--	No Change	
-	-	1	0	LMAR	From LIT	
-	-	1	1	MAR	From BSW	
-	1	0	-	BR2	From BSW	
-	1	1	1	MAR2	From BSW	
1	-	0	-	BR1	From BSW	
1	-	1	1	MAR1	From BSW	

46	47	48		Counter Input	
-	0	0	--	No Change	
0	0	1	LCTR	From LIT*	
1	0	1	CTR	From BSW*	
-	1	0	INC	+1	
-	1	1	?		

*Ones Complement

49	50		SAR Input	
0	0	--	No Change	
0	1	CSAR	Complement	
1	0	SAR	From BSW	
1	1	?		

51	52	53	54		Mem Dev Op--MDOP	
0	0	0	0	--	No Change	
0	0	1	0	MR1		
0	0	1	1	MR2		
0	1	1	0	MW1		
0	1	1	1	MW2		
1	0	0	0	DL1	[ASR]	
1	0	0	1	DL2	[ASE]	
1	0	1	1	DR1		
1	0	1	1	DR2		
1	1	0	0	DU1		
1	1	0	1	DU2		
1	1	1	0	DW1		
1	1	1	1	DW2		
	Others			?		

nanomemory. The microprogram memory is 16 bits wide and contains addresses into the 54-bit wide nanomemory. The difference between this and the Grasselli concept is that the microprogram memory also contains "literal" microinstructions which are used directly without reference to the nanomemory. Micro and nano control formats are illustrated in Figure 3-7. This *split* control store is quite different from *levels* of control store as in the QM-1.

A still different concept of multiple levels has been examined by Tsuchiya and Ramamoorthy. They discuss a hierarchy of levels related to the access speeds of the memories involved and reserve the term *control store* for the level of memory out of which microprograms actually *execute;* other levels of microprogram memory may be used for *storage* of microprograms. In addition to the control store (also called the *control cache*), microprograms may be stored in an intermediate *secondary cache* or *microprogram buffer,* or in the main memory itself. The path from the main memory to the control store is through the microprogram buffer. In addition to their design for this multilevel architecture, Tsuchiya and Ramamoorthy have developed algorithms for the optimum (cost-performance) allocation of microprograms to the different storage levels in accordance with their execution frequencies and the speeds of the memories.[16]

To date, the two-level machine concept (Grasselli, QM-1) has primarily been utilized for its capabilities in microprogramming research. Potentially it can be exploited to provide effective compromise solutions to the many trade-offs involved. *Hard* nanoprogramming can be utilized to effect a limited tailoring of the microprogrammable architecture to support a target machine emulation, while *soft* microprogramming can make the actual task of writing the emulator easier. Powerful (and hence dangerous) capabilities of horizontal microprogramming can be restricted to a privileged mode, while higher level microprogram capabilities are freely available to the user. In short, a two-level control store structure has many advantages; its prime disadvantage lies in the fact that the additional level also adds additional delay and increases macro-execution (emulation) time.

---

[16] See TSUC72, bibliography.

3.7 SUMMARY

This chapter has introduced many of the design alternatives and parameters associated with microprogrammable machines. Although each topic has been discussed independently, in practice there is considerable overlap between them. Some of the more significant characteristics that relate to the popular horizontal/vertical classification of processors were presented and summarized in Figure 3-3.

Many examples have been cited of microprogrammable computers having specific features or employing particular design concepts. References have been provided in the footnotes for those interested in more detailed study of any of the architectures mentioned.

In the following chapters, four commercially available microprogrammable computers are examined in depth. These machines have been selected on the basis of their representing significantly different microprogrammable architectures. Additionally, summary descriptions of other popular or otherwise interesting architectures, including examples of microprogrammable microprocessors, are presented in the concluding chapter.

Chapter 4

Microdata 3200 Architecture

4.0 SUMMARY DESCRIPTION

The Microdata 3200 processor is a general purpose microprogrammable computer capable of handling data widths of 8 and 16 bits. Working storage is provided by three 16-bit registers (X, Y, and Z) supplemented by two banks of general purpose file registers, each containing 16 registers. In addition, the file registers and several special purpose registers have been designed to implement a stack head for support of stack operations. Other special purpose register facilities are provided to directly support target machine emulation.

Microinstructions are 32 bits in length and are essentially vertical in that they control a single functional operation at a time. Each microinstruction determines the address of its successor. Up to 4K words of control store are available, either read-only or read-write. Dynamic microprogramming is possible.

4.1 3200 SYSTEM

The Microdata 3200 is not only a general purpose microprogrammable machine, but it has facilities provided which enhance its use as a general purpose emulator as well. At least two different emulators are available from the manufacturer which tailor the micro level architecture to perform as considerably different target machines.

At the system level it is possible to configure many different systems, depending on the number and type of modules selected (Figure 4-1). The simplest configuration includes a single module of each of the three principal module types, processor, input/output,

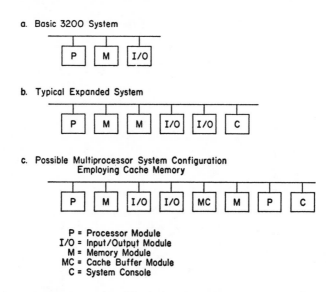

Fig. 4-1: Representative Microdata 3200 System Configuration.

and memory, as shown in Figure 4-1a. Intermodule connection is via a centralized high speed *Monobus*.

4.2 3200 PROCESSOR

The architecture of the 3200 CPU is illustrated in the block diagram of Figure 4-2. It is primarily a 16-bit machine with a generous amount of useful local store registers, including a stack capability. Control is more vertical in nature than horizontal, although it has some aspects of both. Only the principal registers and units are shown in the figure.

4.2.1 Processing Facilities

ALU

The major processing facility of the 3200 processor is the arithmetic logic unit (ALU). Capable of operating in either byte (8-bit) or word (16-bit) mode, the ALU performs addition and subtraction, data transfer, complementation, and logical AND, OR, exclusive-OR, and implication functions. The arithmetic convention is 2's comple-

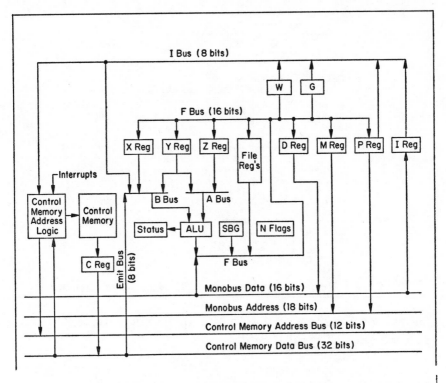

Fig. 4-2: Microdata 3200 CPU Block Diagram.

ment. It is possible to either enable or inhibit an input carry or borrow from the previous (less significant) operation under microprogram control.

Inputs to the ALU are from the A bus and/or the B bus as shown in the figure. Output is always via the F bus to a selected destination register. Operations are normally in 16-bit word mode unless one of the allowable byte register destination codes is specified (X register upper or lower byte, Z register upper byte, D Register upper or lower byte), automatically causing the ALU to operate in byte mode.

Arithmetic Status

Two sets of status registers are available, each including carry, overflow, negative, and zero bits. The F (firmware flags) register may be enabled to set these four bits according to the actual conditions generated by the ALU. The second set (TFG) is used for representation of target machine conditions and may either be set according to the F bits or, alternatively, may be set from the lowest four bits of the Z register. This is one example of special emulation support facilities provided in the 3200 architecture.

Shifting

Shifts of 1 bit may be performed on a byte, word, or double word (32 bits). For greater than 1-bit shifts, repetitive single-bit shifts must be executed in the microprogram. Shifts are accomplished in any of the ALU working registers (X, Y, Z). Any of the three may be used for full word shifts, while the X and Z both have byte shift capabilities. The Y and Z registers may be used together for 32-bit double word (or two independent full word) shifts. The bit position(s) vacated by a shift may be filled with a 0, 1, or a bit being shifted out, thus permitting a wide variation of shift types including arithmetic, logical, and circular.

4.2.2 Local Store Facilities

Working Registers

The X, Y, and Z ALU working registers have already been mentioned. X and Z are byte addressable and the Y register may be selected as either the A bus or B bus input to the ALU. Any of these three working registers may serve as the ALU output destination.

File Registers

The file registers (FR) consist of two banks of sixteen registers, each 16 bits long, that can function as high-speed general purpose local memory. In addition, the first four registers of the primary FR bank are organized to function as part of a push-down stack head, and the last six registers of the primary bank can influence the setting of the high order bits (18, 17) of the monobus address register (M reg) (see section 4.3).

A file register can serve as either a source or a destination, but only one or the other during any one microinstruction execution cycle. Selecting an FR as a source register activates its associated bank as the currently active bank, and subsequent destinations in the FR must be within the same bank. A 4-bit bus is used to index into either bank of the file registers. It can be driven from a variety of sources including control memory, Z reg, and G reg.

Stack Facilities

A series of features are provided that contribute to a powerful stack capability in the 3200 processor. These include the four file registers in the primary bank previously discussed, a T-counter (not shown), and the Y and N registers. The Y register and file registers function together as a stack head, with the Y register as the top of the stack. Up to four additional words complete the stack head in the file registers, while unlimited additional stack words can be placed in main memory. The T-counter keeps track of the file register that contains the second word in the stack; operating as a cyclic modulo 4 counter, it eliminates the need to physically move data between file registers when the stack is pushed or popped. Since it is possible that less than five words may be in the stack head at any time, the N register indicates the number of active words. It functions as a 5-bit shift register with consecutive 1's indicating active stack words and 0's indicating inactive words in the stack head. The high order N bit corresponds to the top of the stack (Y reg), the next bit the second stack word as pointed to by the T-counter, and the remaining bits correspond to the remaining stack head file registers in cyclic sequence. Actual pushing and popping requires microprogram routines, but these facilities greatly facilitate the actions.

Figure 4-3 illustrates a snapshot of a possible stack situation. As is usually the case, Y reg is the top of the stack. The T-counter points to FR 02 (primary bank) as the second word in the stack head. Since there are four high order 1's in the N reg, this indicates that a total of four words are active in the stack head; hence, two additional file registers are active, which are 03 and 00 (cyclic sequence) and FR 01 does not currently contain an active stack word. The next stack word after FR 00 and all other words in the stack would be in main memory. (The microprogrammer would be required to maintain a pointer to the current top of the stack body in main memory, in addition to controlling detailed stack manipulations.)

Memory Access Registers

The D register serves as a "destination" register capable of sending information out on the data portion of the Monobus for transfer to

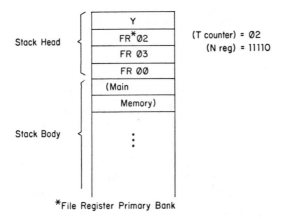

Fig. 4-3: A Snapshot of a Typical Stack and
Associated Register Contents.

main memory or through an I/O module to an output device. It functions in this manner in conjunction with the M register (18 bits) which can similarly be loaded with an address to be applied to the address portion of the Monobus (least significant 16 bits). These registers, then, normally play key roles in input/output or main memory accesses.

Another example of facilities designed to aid the 3200 in the emulation of other machines is the P and I register set. These registers are similar in some respects to the M and D registers, but they are intended specifically to be used in the emulation of a target machine's program location counter (P reg, 18 bits) and instruction register (I). Like the M register, P reg can gate an address onto the address portion of the Monobus, as in the fetch of a target machine instruction from main memory. The fetched instruction then is held in the I reg, from which it may be gated onto I bus a byte at a time and thence to either the ALU or the control unit to effect branching to target instruction execution microroutines.

An incrementing capability is included in P reg to enhance its function as a typical program location counter. Whenever it is incremented to an even address (corresponding to a 16-bit word in the byte addressable main memory), or loaded with new data from the F bus, a main memory read into the I reg is automatically initiated to effect fetch of the next target instruction. Generally, this can result in an overlap of target instruction fetch and execute cycles for improved emulation efficiency.

Other Registers

A single bit generator (SBG) is available for special mask and constant generation. Its function is to activate one of the 16-bit lines of the F bus with a 1, placing 0's on all of the others.

The general indicator register (G) is a 4-bit register that can be set under microprogram control, as can the self-decrementing W-counter, also 4 bits in length. Both of these facilities have utility in the control of microinstruction sequencing operations that will be examined further in this chapter in section 4.2.4.

In addition to the registers mentioned here, a number of other special purchase registers are included in the 3200. These will be discussed along with the specific features to which they pertain.

4.2.3 Control Store

Control memory for the 3200 processor is organized into 32-bit words, each containing a single microinstruction. Only one level is utilized. Maximum size of the control memory is 4K words. Since only 2K words (read-only) can be contained on the same physical board holding the remainder of the control unit, control memory address and data buses are indicated in Figure 4-2 and would be employed with additional control memory boards.

The 4K (maximum) words of control memory are divided into eight pages, with each page containing 16 "blocks" of 16 two-word microinstruction "pairs" each. The significance of these groupings will be examined in the discussion of microinstruction sequencing (4.2.4).

Either read-only or read-write control store can be utilized. The hardware does support control store writing under microprogram control; thus, dynamic microprogramming is possible with this machine.

4.2.4 Microinstructions

Format

The 32-bit microinstruction is divided into nine encoded fields as shown in Figure 4-4. The descriptive names in the figure oversimplify

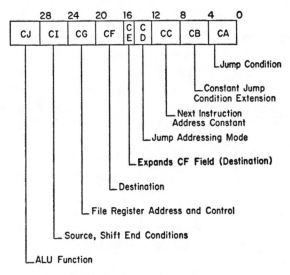

Fig. 4-4: Microinstruction Format.

the functions performed by many of these fields, since in addition to the encoding within fields, the exact function performed by a field may be conditioned according to the contents of another field. A significant amount of flexibility has been sacrificed in order to reduce the control word size to 32 bits. If a longer control word had been utilized, it would not have been necessary to preclude simultaneous control access over facilities not otherwise mutually exclusive within the hardware (such as the restriction on file registers not being both a source and a destination within the same microinstruction). Of course, a longer control word would mean a commensurate increase in control memory size (total bits) and hence cost, and could well result in lower efficiency control memory utilization and increased microprogramming difficulty. Such are the trade-offs faced by every designer.

Operations

The CE, CF, CG, CI, and CJ fields together form the operative portion of the microinstruction, specifying the processing function to be accomplished and source and destination registers to be utilized. Additionally, the CB field may contain constant (immediate) data to be input to the ALU, or extended control information assisting the CJ, CI, or CG fields. Facilities and options available were covered in sections 4.2.1 and 4.2.2.

Sequencing

In effect, each microinstruction contains the address of its successor, with a considerable number of alternative jump options depending on testable conditions. The organization of control memory into pages (up to 8 of 512 words each), blocks (16 per page), and microinstruction pairs (16 per block) was described in section 4.2.3, and the format of a complete 12-bit control memory address is illustrated in Figure 4-5. This subdividing of control memory allows fewer than a full 12 bits to be utilized within a microinstruction to provide meaningful branches within pairs, blocks, and pages as will be described.

A 12-bit Last Access Register (L reg) holds the address of the microinstruction currently being executed. In addition a 16-bit Save Register (S reg) is available for either saving the current (or modified) L contents for use in returning from a subroutine, or, alternatively, it may be used to receive data from the F bus. S reg contents can then be used in developing an address for subsequent control memory access.

The jump addressing mode for each microinstruction is contained in the 4-bit CD field. The mode thus selected limits the resulting range of jumps available to as low as a block or as high as the entire control memory. In almost every mode, the CA field (and possibly the CB field also) specifies a jump condition that will be tested to determine the word within a pair of possible successor microinstructions. The CC field may further specify the pair, block, or page; and in some modes, the CB field may be used (in addition to the CC field which specifies a block) to select a pair as well. Finally, two modes are available that allow branching according to the first or second 4-bit digit on the I bus (target instruction decoding) or in response to pending interrupt signals.

Over 30 possible test conditions can be called for according to the contents of the CA field (and frequently CB also). These primarily allow testing of various conditions in the self-decrementing W-counter (loop control), N register (stack manipulation), key bits in the X, Y, and Z ALU staging registers, arithmetic flags (AF), and the general indicator (G reg). Other testable conditions include key bits in the S register and first and second I bus digits to facilitate subroutine returns and target instruction decoding respectively.

The branching facilities provided readily permit complex branch-

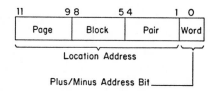

Fig. 4-5: Control Memory Address Format.

ing operations. An example is the Next Operation Branch which can be performed following completion of a microroutine used for the emulation of a target machine instruction. In this case, a 48-way conditional branch is executed. The first 16 choices are based on possible interrupt conditions, both internal and external; if no interrupt conditions are present, a 32-way branch is executed based on the first four bits of the current target instruction (I reg, gated onto I bus) and a selectable jump condition.

Interrupts

An 8-bit Q register is available and setable from the F bus to mask selected interrupt conditions. Further control over interrupts is provided in that they can only be invoked through use of the First Digit Branch control memory accessing mode as specified in the CD field. If emulation is not being done in a particular microprogram, or if the target machine instructions are such that decoding is best accomplished by a method other than through utilization of the first digit branch, then such microinstructions must be included solely for the purpose of interrupt response. Thus, interrupt handling in the Microdata 3200 is *soft* in the fullest sense and requires a great deal of caution on the part of the microprogrammer.

Microprogramming

Depending on the nature of the target machine being emulated and its instruction word format in particular, the 3200 architecture as controlled by available microinstruction parameters may well enable highly efficient emulation microprograms. It must be recognized, however, that at least in some cases (unusual instruction formats, field lengths, placements, and so on) it may be necessary to "defeat" some of the 3200 hardware functions, with a resulting loss of efficiency.

The 32-bit microinstruction length places the 3200 somewhere in between what can clearly be considered short word and long word machines. The degree of encoding employed and the single controllable operation per microinstruction make the machine look generally vertical, while the number of fields and their functions are more horizontal in nature. To be sure, microprogramming the pure hardware machine is not a simple task. The careful reader will have noted, for instance, a number of potentially conflicting uses of the CB field that might necessitate two or more microinstructions in lieu of one (longer) microinstruction to accomplish a given action. Nevertheless, a great deal of power is available to the microprogrammer through the microinstruction capabilities provided.

4.3 MAIN MEMORY, INPUT/OUPUT, AND THE MONOBUS

External Data Access

The Monobus was shown in Figure 4-1 to be the vehicle for intermodule communication. Hence all input/output operations or main memory reads-writes called for by the processor are accomplished over the Monobus.

In Figure 4-2 the Monobus is seen to be subdivided into a 16-bit Monobus Data bus and an 18-bit Monobus Address bus. The 18 bits provide for a total addressing capability of 256K unique addresses. The upper 16K addresses are reserved for I/O controllers and devices, with the remainder available for main memory (229,376 bytes). Since memory is byte addressable, the low order bit specifies a byte within the two-byte word size.

Both the P and M registers are 18 bits in length and can thus address the full address space available. Two small registers, each 2 bits long, are available for use in generating the upper 2 bits of an 18-bit address. These can be set from the F bus and then gated into M reg prior to a Monobus data access. In addition, one of these extender registers can receive the upper two most significant bits from the P reg to pass to the M reg when any of the last six file registers in the primary bank are accessed, enhancing the utility of these file registers as pointers into main memory (that is, as program counters, stack pointers, and so on).

Monobus Features

Module selection by the Monobus can be overlapped with the previous data transfer operation. Priority polling is used to determine which module will have control for the next transfer operation, and priority interrupt lines are provided for communication from the Monobus to processors.

All bus transfers, regardless of modules involved, are fully asynchronous; therefore, it is possible to replace modules with functionally equivalent modules having improved performance characteristics (such as faster memory) as technology evolves, and the system can take full advantage of the resulting speed benefits. In this same manner, a cache memory can be employed to reduce time lost waiting for data to be read from main memory; the cache will automatically abort the normal memory read when it detects a read from a location indicated as present in its directory.

DMA

The ability of I/O modules to initiate Monobus cycles in the same manner as processors results in an inherent direct memory access (DMA) capability.

4.4 ORGANIZATIONAL PARAMETERS

The present generation of 3200 system modules employ state-of-the-art technology with commensurate performance. Control memory access time, for example, is 60 nanoseconds with a complete control memory cycle time of 135 nanoseconds. This same interval is the full cycle time of the synchronous CPU. Main memory accesses into the MOS semiconductor memory module require 350 nanoseconds, with a full read cycle taking 500 nanoseconds.

4.5 SUMMARY

The Microdata 3200 has both a modular system level architecture and a CPU structure particularly well suited to emulation. Emulators already exist that enable the 3200 to emulate the Microdata 800 and

1600 series (marketed as the 3230), and also a new 32/S stack oriented target machine, designed as an efficient high level language processor.

The 3200 is certainly well suited to general purpose micro-programming in addition to emulation. To ease the burden on the microprogrammer, a full assembler CAP 32 is available.

Chapter 5

Interdata 8/32 Micro Level Architecture

5.0 SUMMARY DESCRIPTION

The Interdata Model 8/32 is a 32-bit machine with a 3-bus architecture (A/B source, S destination). From two to eight *sets* of 16 general registers each are available, plus an additional set of 16 registers dedicated to floating point operations and eight registers reserved for microprogram use. The 32-bit ALU also includes hardware floating point capabilities. Microinstructions are of the vertical type with six general formats. Execution is normally sequential with explicit branching microinstructions available. Control store (partially read-write) words are 32 bits in length, each containing a single microinstruction. Main memory, accessed via a memory bus, is also 32 bits wide, but is byte addressable. In addition to regular memory address and data registers, special registers are provided to serve as the user (target) level instruction register and location counter, the latter as part of a program status word. Many features are tailored for emulation of the user level Interdata architecture and are limited in their general utility.

5.1 INTRODUCTION

The Interdata 8/32 micro level architecture is included in this book as a representative of the class of microprogrammable machines that have been designed with the primary purpose of implementing a particular machine language level architecture, but can also support limited general purpose microprogramming as well. As a minimum, such machines should be capable of extending the existing macroinstruction repertoire through add-on microcode in read-write control store; ideally, sufficient read-write control store will be available to permit substitution of a completely different emulator or comparable size microprogram. The latter is partially the case with the Interdata 8/32 micro level architecture, although emulation capabilities are somewhat restricted as will be seen.

There are strong similarities between the Model 8/32 micro level architecture and the 8/32 user level architecture. This becomes especially apparent when one considers that most 8/32 user level instructions can be emulated with one or two micro level instructions. In effect, the micro level architecture is to a large extent an extension of the user level architecture.

It may also be useful to know that the micro level architecture of the Model 8/32 is very similar to that of the earlier Model 80 micro level machine, or, more specifically, the Model 85, which provides dynamic control store capabilities to support user microprogramming. Of course, the Model 80 series processors are 16-bit machines, do not include hardware floating point features, and have fewer registers available. Since the microinstruction repertoires of the Model 85 and 8/32 are very similar, many of the differences between the two are transparent to the microprogrammer, their primary effect being in performance rather than functional capabilities.

To fully utilize the 8/32 micro level architecture for general purpose microprogramming, the microprogrammer should have a basic understanding of the 8/32 user level architecture (Figure 5-1) and instruction set. This is true because of unique hardware features designed to facilitate 8/32 user level instruction emulation; these features must be either utilized to advantage or in some way defeated by the microprogrammer, since they are controllable only to a minimum extent. These hardware features and their relationship to the 8/32 user level architecture will be discussed along with the appropriate sections to which they pertain.

5.2 MODEL 8/32 HARDWARE

A block diagram of the Model 8/32 micro level hardware is shown in Figure 5-2. Significant features include the 32-bit wide data paths and arithmetic processing facilities, the three major buses (A, B, S), and the dedicated (emulation) control hardware facilities and asso-

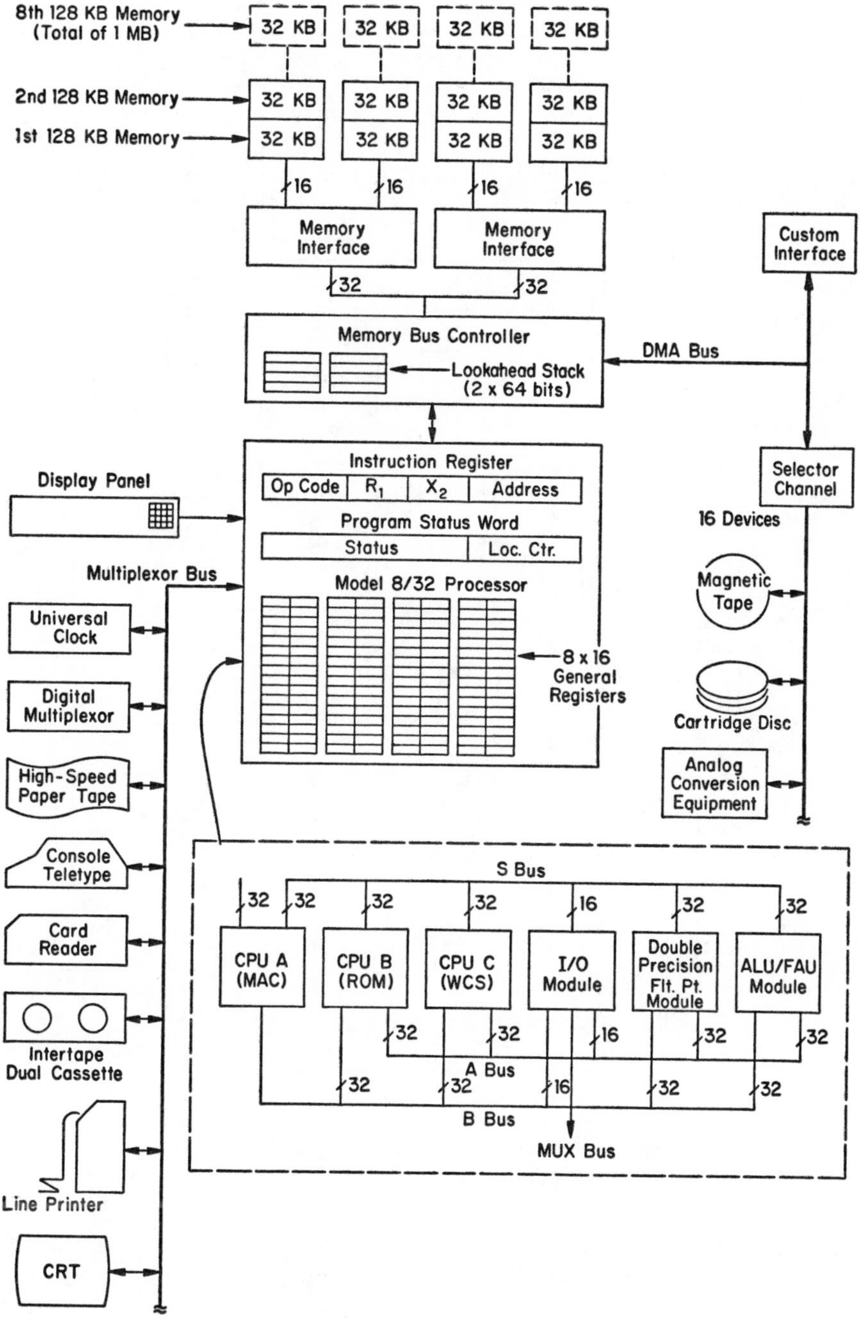

Fig. 5-1: Model 8/32 User Level Processor Block Diagram
(Courtesy Interdata Inc.).

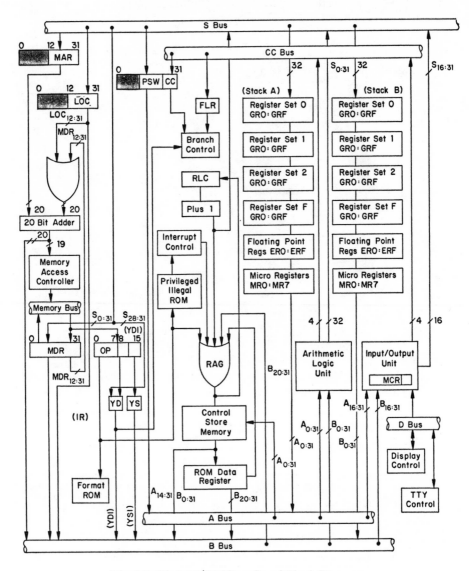

Fig. 5-2: Model 8/32 Micro Level Block Diagram
(Courtesy Interdata Inc.).

ciated registers. Special buses are also provided to accommodate
condition code movement (CC bus), input/output operations (D
bus), and main memory operations (memory bus). While 32 bits
make up the normal word length, both halfword (16 bits) and byte
(8 bits) operations are also available.

5.2.1 Processing Facilities

ALU

The primary processing facility available in the 8/32 is the 32-bit arithmetic logic unit (ALU). Inputs to the ALU are from the 32-bit A (first operand) and B (second operand) buses; arithmetic output is via the 32-bit S bus, while resultant condition code output is available on the 4-bit CC bus, including carry (C), overflow (V), greater than zero (G), and less than zero (L).

The ALU performs the arithmetic operations of addition, subtraction, multiplication, and division on fixed point 32-bit operands, as well as a variety of shift (logical and arithmetic) and rotate operations. Arithmetic and logical shifts can also be performed on half-words. Logical operations possible include AND, OR, and exclusive-OR. Two's complement convention is utilized throughout for handling negative operands.

Floating Point ALU

The 8/32 arithmetic logic unit is also capable of performing floating point arithmetic operations using single precision floating point operands. Format for floating point operands is indicated in Figure 5-3. A 24-bit signed fraction (radix point is assumed to be to the left of bit 8, the high order fraction bit) is raised to the power of 16 determined from the exponent field. The 7-bit exponent is expressed in excess 64 notation; thus, the true exponent value is obtained by subtracting 64 from the absolute value indicated in the 7-bit binary exponent field. Operations available include multiplication and division, addition and subtraction, unnormalized addition, compare, and "compare and equalize" which unnormalizes the smaller of the two operands to effectively align the two radix points.

5.2.2 Local Store

General Registers

From two to eight full sets of 16 general registers each (GR0–GRF) may be available in the 8/32 processor.[1] Each register set is

---

[1] Set F shown in Figure 5-2 is actually set 7, for consistency with previous Interdata notations.

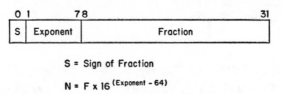

S = Sign of Fraction

$N = F \times 16^{(Exponent - 64)}$

Fig. 5-3: Model 8/32 Floating Point Format.

duplicated for the A and B buses (stack A and stack B in Figure 5-2); the duplication permits independent concurrent accessing of the registers by the two buses, but in actuality they behave in effect as single sets and the duplication is transparent to the micropro-grammer/programmer. (The term *stack* as used by the manufacturer may be misleading here since the general registers do not function as push-down stacks in the accepted sense of the term.)

The general register sets are intended for use at the macro-machine level, and in fact are all available as part of the 8/32 user (macro) level architecture. Of course, they are directly accessible to the micro-programmer as well. Only one 16-register set is active at any one time, as selected by 3 bits in the program status word (see below and Table 5-1). This is a powerful feature which, for instance, can enhance system performance in a multiprogramming mode since the contents of an entire register set can remain intact and not require temporary storage when another program is given control. Alterna-tively, they may be used to support multilevel programming and nested blocks.

General registers may be addressed either directly or indirectly. Indirect addressing facilitates emulation by allowing the micro-programmer to call for the general register(s) specified in the user level instruction (see YD and YS fields in the instruction register below) without having to evaluate the register specification fields in the user's instruction.

Floating Point Registers

In addition to the regular general register sets discussed above, a full set of 16 floating point registers (ER0–ERF) is also provided, dedicated for use with the floating point ALU operations. Like the general registers, they are intended for user level usage and may be addressed directly or indirectly. The floating point registers are not

Table 5-1: Program Status Word Key Bits*
(Courtesy Interdata Inc.).

BIT	MEANING
14 15 16	
17	Interrupt Priority Selection (w/bit 20)
18	Machine Malfunction Interrupt Enable
19	
20	Interrupt Priority Selection (w/bit 17)
21	Relocation/Protection Interrupt Enable
22	
23	Privileged/Protect Mode
24	

25
26
27
	Selects
	     Active
	         General Register Set

28 29 30 31	C—Carry V—Overflow } Condition G—Greater than Zero } Codes L—Less than Zero

*Blank entries have no hardware signifi-
cance and are defined only by the emulator.

distinguishable from the general registers by explicit address; instead, they simply become the active set of registers (overriding the PSW designated set) whenever a floating point arithmetic microinstruction is being executed. Thus, an A bus register designation of 00010 will select ER2 for a floating point microinstruction or GR2 (active set) for any other microinstruction. In some ways this scheme limits flexibility since the direct manipulation of data in the floating point registers is restricted to that which can be explicitly accomplished using the eight available floating point microinstructions.

Microregisters

A special set of eight 32-bit general purpose registers (MR0–MR7) is provided for the exclusive use of the microprogrammer. They are explicitly (and directly) addressable in addition to the active set of general registers.

It should be noted that floating point arithmetic microinstructions may utilize the microregisters as well as the floating point registers; hence, the microregisters can provide a link between the floating point registers and the general registers, or permit indirect manipulation of data in the floating point registers beyond the basic capabilities of the floating point microinstructions if the requirement arises. A number of microinstructions would be required to effect the necessary transfers and processing, but the capability does exist to at least partially offset the limitations on floating point register accessibility.

Instruction Register

The instruction register (IR) is one of several hardware features provided that is designed specifically for support of the emulation of the user level 8/32 instruction set and not readily generalizable to other emulations. The IR is comprised of three subregisters, OP which contains bits 0–7 of a user level 8/32 instruction, YD which contains bits 8–11, and YS which contains bits 12–15. Together then, the three subregisters hold a 16-bit halfword; complete 8/32 instructions may be 16, 32, or 48 bits in length and may thus require additional memory fetches as will be discussed below.

User level 8/32 instruction formats are indicated in Figure 5-4. In all cases the user level operation code occupies bits 0–7 and will therefore be available in the OP register. Similarly, bits 8–11 always specify a user level general (or floating point) register, while bits 12–15 specify either a user level general (or floating point) register or a 4-bit immediate operand. The YD and YS registers thus provide the capability for indirectly addressing general and floating point registers within microinstructions; specification within a microinstruction of YD or YS in lieu of a specific general register will cause the microinstruction to utilize the register pointed to by YD or YS from the user level instruction.

Memory control facilities are discussed in section 5.2.4. For the time being it is sufficient to state that one of the memory control

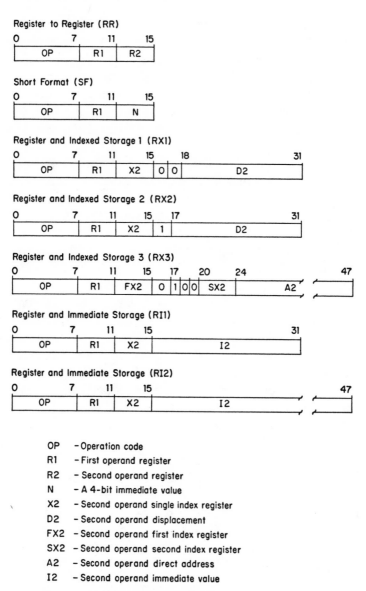

OP   – Operation code
R1   – First operand register
R2   – Second operand register
N   – A 4-bit immediate value
X2   – Second operand single index register
D2   – Second operand displacement
FX2   – Second operand first index register
SX2   – Second operand second index register
A2   – Second operand direct address
I2   – Second operand immediate value

Fig. 5-4: User Level Model 8/32 Instruction Formats
(Courtesy Interdata Inc.).

options available to the microprogrammer is to specify an Instruction
Read operation. This will result in a halfword (as addressed by LOC
described below) being fetched and placed in the OP register and its

8-bit extension as shown in Figure 5-2. YD and YS are not loaded at this time, but the data that will subsequently be transferred into YD and YS are held in the 8-bit OP extension.

Execution of an Instruction Read sets in motion a chain of events employing user level 8/32 dedicated hardware support features. Loading of the OP register causes an automatic table look-up operation using the Format ROM shown in Figure 5-2. The 8-bit OP code is used as an address to select one of the 256 four-bit ROM words that indicate the user level 8/32 instruction format in accordance with the codes shown in Table 5-2a. Based on the user level instruction and data contained in the format ROM, additional halfwords are automatically fetched as required and placed in the memory data register. Resulting contents of the MDR and B bus are illustrated in Figure 5-5. It is readily apparent then that this automatic hardware support is tailored specifically to the user level 8/32 architecture.

Separate from the Instruction Read memory control action, the microprogrammer can initiate a Decode Next User Instruction action. This also sets in motion a chain of events to facilitate user level 8/32 emulation. First, interrupts are checked for (see section 5.4). At this time, if no interrupts are pending, the YD and YS registers are updated from the 8-bit OP register extension. Once again a 256-word ROM is interrogated in a table look-up operation to check the possible Privileged/Illegal status of the OP code being decoded. Each ROM word again contains 4 bits whose meanings are indicated in Table 5-2b. Any of the three illegal instruction bits will cause an abort of the instruction fetch/decode and result in an illegal instruction interrupt. If the privileged instruction bit is set, then bit 23 of the PSW determines the subsequent action; if it is a 1, the illegal instruction interrupt occurs, while if it is a 0, decode and execution are permitted to continue. Assuming a legal user level 8/32 instruction OP code is present, twice the OP code will be used as the control store address to enter the execution portion of the emulation routine.

In summary, the Instruction Register and the associated Format ROM and Privileged/Illegal ROM in a standard Model 8/32 are tailored exclusively to the user level 8/32 emulation. These facilities are activated by using the microinstruction commands Instruction Read and Decode Next User Instruction. Their use greatly simplifies user level 8/32 emulation and results in high emulation efficiency.

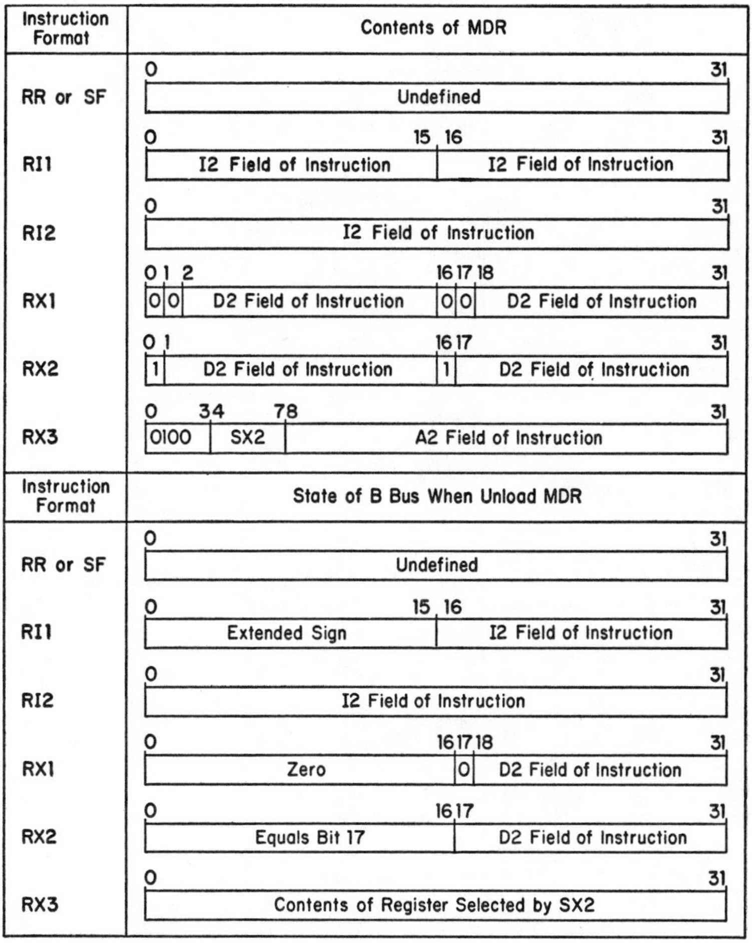

Instruction Format	Contents of MDR		
RR or SF	0 Undefined 31		
RI1	0 15 16 31 I2 Field of Instruction | I2 Field of Instruction		
RI2	0 31 I2 Field of Instruction		
RX1	0 1 2 16 17 18 31 |0|0| D2 Field of Instruction |0|0| D2 Field of Instruction		
RX2	0 1 16 17 31 |1| D2 Field of Instruction |1| D2 Field of Instruction		
RX3	0 3 4 7 8 31 |0100| SX2 | A2 Field of Instruction		
Instruction Format	State of B Bus When Unload MDR		
RR or SF	0 Undefined 31		
RI1	0 15 16 31 Extended Sign | I2 Field of Instruction		
RI2	0 31 I2 Field of Instruction		
RX1	0 16 17 18 31 Zero |0| D2 Field of Instruction		
RX2	0 16 17 31 Equals Bit 17 | D2 Field of Instruction		
RX3	0 31 Contents of Register Selected by SX2		

Fig. 5-5: Contents of MDR after a User Lever 8/32 Instruction Read
(Courtesy Interdata Inc.).

Without hardware modification, emulation of other macro level architectures must be accomplished without using these features/ commands and with considerable loss of efficiency.

Program Status Word

The 32-bit program status word (PSW) is used to indicate status of the machine relative to the current user level program. Only bits 14–31 are actually implemented. The functions of key bits are indicated in Table 5-1; these all have hardware significance, while the

Table 5-2: Decode ROM's for User Level 8/32 Instructions (Courtesy Interdata Inc.).

Contents				Format
1	0	0	0	RX
0	0	0	1	RI1
0	1	0	0	RI2
0	0	1	0	RR (Short)
0	0	0	0	Undefined

a. Contents of Format ROM Words and Their Interpretation as User Level Formats.

Contents				Meaning
1				Illegal Instruction: Model 8/32 w/Double Precision Floating Point
	1			Illegal Instruction: Model 8/32 w/Floating Point
		1		Illegal Instruction: Basic Model 8/32
			1	Privileged Instruction

b. Contents of Privileged/Illegal ROM Words and Their Meanings.

remainder (blank in Table 5-1) are defined only by the emulator. Bits 28–31 constitute the condition code of the user level program. The microprogrammer has the choice of allowing these to be directly updated from the CC bus at the conclusion of each arithmetic or I/O operation (E field of microinstruction enables this) or he may directly control their contents by explicitly addressing the PSW as a destination register. The location counter (LOC) discussed below may be considered as an extension of the PSW; together, the two registers indicate the complete status of the current user level program.

Flag Register

The 4-bit flag register (FLR) is the hardware implementation of the 4 condition code bits (C, V, G, L). These bits are always set according to the results of the last microinstruction executed; the same information may or may not be gated to the CC portion of the PSW as the microprogrammer desires.

A full set of branching microinstructions is available to test the status of individual FLR bits. In addition, the CC field in the PSW may be tested for a match with the user instruction R1 field (bits 8—11) to support similar user level branching instructions.

Location Counter

The last of the registers designed to support user level 8/32 emulation is the location counter (LOC). While logically 32 bits in length, only bits 12—31 are physically implemented, allowing for an address space of 1M bytes of directly addressable memory.

Functionally, the LOC points to the main memory address of the next user level instruction. It is this register that is used to select the main memory location when the Instruction Read memory command is included in the microinstruction. Thus, use of the LOC is tied in with the loading of the IR (OP, YD, YS) as previously discussed and is therefore limited in its general utility.

The LOC may be automatically incremented, either independently or in conjunction with an instruction read. (The full range of options is detailed later in Table 5-4). Incrementation is always by the total number of bytes in the last user level instruction.

Machine Control Register

The machine control register (MCR) that is shown in the I/O unit of Figure 5-2 is a 12-bit register (only 10 bits are used) that contains indicators of internal and external conditions, including some of the interrupt conditions to be discussed in section 5.4. It can be both interrogated and cleared under microprogram control.

5.2.3 Control Store

Control store words are 32 bits long, each containing a single microinstruction. Maximum size is 4K words, organized into 16 pages of 256 words each. The standard Model 8/32 includes five pages or a total of 1,280 words of control store implemented in read-only memory (ROM) and containing the complete user level 8/32 emulator. Eleven pages are optionally available as writeable control store (or dynamic control store in the manufacturer's terminology).

Control store addresses are 12 bits in length. Locations are addressed by the output of the ROM address gate (RAG) which has several possible inputs. User level 8/32 instruction emulation, previously discussed, may provide a source of address selection based on decoding of the OP field, or an illegal instruction interrupt. Alternatively, the ROM location counter (RLC), selected bits of the ROM data register (also called the ROM instruction register), and the B bus may be used to provide addresses. The latter two sources permit a variety of branching and data addressing options.

Output of the control store is normally to the ROM instruction register. When control store words are accessed for *data* to be used as *operands,* such access is accomplished indirectly. Setting of a control bit (I) in the microinstruction results in what would normally be an *operand* itself (register contents or immediate microinstruction field on the B bus), being instead utilized as a control store *address;* the contents of this control store address becomes the actual operand.

Writing into the control store is accomplished directly with the data to be written taken from the A bus and the address taken from the B bus.

5.2.4 Main Memory

Main memory for the Model 8/32 is available in 128K-byte modules up to a maximum of 1M bytes of directly addressable storage. The memory bus accepts commands from the current microinstruction. Operation of the memory is asynchronous, allowing the microprogram to continue execution while the memory operation is being completed. Attempting to access data before a read is complete, for example, merely causes the processor to wait until the read has been completed.

Memory Data Register

The memory data register (MDR) serves as a data buffer for both memory read and memory write operations. In the special case of an

Instruction Read operation, however, the instruction register (OP, YD, YS) is utilized for the first halfword read, and the resulting MDR contents are as indicated in Figure 5-5, as previously discussed (section 5.2.2, Instruction Register). Output of the MDR is to the B bus (memory reads) and input to the MDR is from the S bus (memory writes).

Memory Address Register

Addresses for accesses to main memory normally come from the memory address register (MAR). Again, in the special case of an Instruction Read, the location counter (LOC) performs the same function.

The 20-bit adder shown in Figure 5-2 is another feature aimed at facilitating user level 8/32 emulation. Specifically, it is called into play for effective address generation for operand fetch in the emulation of complex user level addressing modes. Functioning of the adder is invoked automatically during the Decode Next User Instruction operation according to the contents of the instruction register and MDR (second and third halfwords of user instruction), and the output of the format ROM. Further, additional hardware may cause the MAR contents to be replaced by the sum of the general register specified by the user instruction X2 field and the MDR contents (RX1 and RX2 formats), or the sum of the two general register contents (SX2 and FX2) in the case of RX3 format. The MAR contents may then be passed to the memory access controller (MAC), added to the MDR, or added to the LOC as required.

A complete description of the entire 8/32 emulation operations is beyond the scope of this book. However, this discussion should serve to reemphasize the tailoring of the hardware to user level 8/32 emulation and the care that must be taken when using the machine for general purpose microprogramming. Once again, avoiding the Instruction Read and Decode functions will minimize difficulties.

Memory Functions

The full range of memory control operations will be detailed in the next section which covers the microinstruction repertoire. Operations using the LOC have already been mentioned. General read-write operations are available for both halfwords and fullwords, plus automatic MAR incrementation. Additionally, a set of "privileged" read-write operations are available that disable the memory access controller.

When memory operations are initiated by a microinstruction, they do not actually begin until the remainder of the microinstruction has completed execution. This permits updating of the MAR or MDR within the same microinstruction and then use of the updated contents in the memory operation.

5.3 MODEL 8/32 MICROINSTRUCTIONS AND CONTROL

Microinstructions for the Model 8/32 are essentially of the vertical type. Each microinstruction is 32 bits in length with fields defined according to one of the six formats shown in Figure 5-6.

5.3.1 Microinstruction Fields

Modules

The first 3 bits of a microinstruction select one of the processor *modules* to perform the primary operation for that microinstruction. Module O is considered to be the control module (branches, and so on), module 1 the fixed point ALU, module 2 the I/O module, and module 3 the floating point ALU. Modules are a logical concept for the microprogrammer and are not necessarily physically separable entities.

Functions

The F or function field acts as an OP code field to specify the function that the selected module is to perform; in some cases the F field is extended by the K field (module 1 and module 2 only). Not all F (or F-K) codes are utilized.

Register Select

The A and B fields are used to identify general registers in the active set, microregisters, or special registers to be used as sources on the A and B bus respectively. Similarly, the S field selects a register to be the S bus destination register. Register address assignments are indicated in Table 5-3. Setting of the I bit (indirect) causes the original B bus contents to be used as an address in control store, and

Address Link

0		2	3	4	5	6			10	11			13	14												25	26	27	28				31
000		1	X	T			S				F					Address										E	D		MC				

Register Branch

0	2	3	4	5	6		10	11		13	14			19	20		24	25	26	27	28			31
000	0	X	T		Null			F			▓▓▓▓▓			B			▓	E	F		MC			

Register to Register Transfer

0	2	3	4	5	6		10	11		15	16		19	20		24	25	26				31
Module	0	0	I		S			A			F			B			C	Page Address				

Register to Register Control

0	2	3	4	5	6		10	11		15	16		19	20		24	25	26	27	28		31
Module	0	1	I		S			A			F			B			K	E	D		MC	

Register to Register Immediate

0	2	3	4	5	6		10	11		15	16		19	20						31
Module	1	0	I		S			A			F			Data						

Register Write

0	2	3	4	5	6		10	11		15	16		19	20		24	25	26	27	28		31
001	1	1	I		Null			A			F			B			K	E	D		MC	

Field	Meaning
A	Selects register to be used as first operand.
B	Selects register to be used as second operand.
C	If set, transfer is conditional.
D	Decode next user instruction.
E	Enable setting of condition code.
F	Specifies function of addressed module.
I	B bus data addresses actual data in control store.
K	F field extension.
MC	Memory control field.
S	Selects register to receive the result.
T	If set, item F must be true for transfer, otherwise false.
X	If set, "execute and link," otherwise "branch and link."

Fig. 5-6: Model 8/32 Microinstruction Formats and Field Definitions (Courtesy Interdata Inc.).

the contents of the addressed control store location to be used as the final B bus operand. The E bit enables the resulting CVGL status conditions to be gated into the CC field of the PSW as previously discussed, in addition to being retained in the flag register.

Memory Control

Limited parallelism permits memory control operations to be initiated by most microinstructions. MC field options and their

Table 5-3: Register Addresses (Courtesy Interdata Inc.).

HEX ADDRESS	S Bus	A Bus	B Bus	Category
00	0	0	0	
01	1	1	1	
02	2	2	2	
03	3	3	3	
04	4	4	4	
05	5	5	5	
06	6	6	6	User's
07	7	7	7	General
08	8	8	8	Registers
09	9	9	9	
0A	10	10	10	
0B	11	11	11	
0C	12	12	12	
0D	13	13	13	
0E	14	14	14	
0F	15	15	15	
10	MR0	MR0	MR0	
11	MR1	MR1	MR1	
12	MR2	MR2	MR2	
13	MR3	MR3	MR3	Micro-
14	MR4	MR4	MR4	registers
15	MR5	MR5	MR5	
16	MR6	MR6	MR6	
17	MR7	MR7	MR7	
18	YS	YS	YS	
19	YD	YD	YD	
1A	LOC	YX	LOC	Special
1B	MDR	YDPI	MDR	Purpose
1C	MAR	—	MAR	
1D	PSW	PSW	YSI	
1E	YDI	—	YDI	
1F	NULL	NULL	NULL	

Note: For floating point instructions, corresponding floating point registers are selected instead of general registers.

meanings are detailed in Table 5-4. If the Instruction Read option is selected, the microprogrammer may either initiate the decode actions by setting the D bit in the same microinstruction, or he may do so in a subsequent microinstruction.

Table 5-4: Memory Control Options (Courtesy Interdata Inc.).

MICROINSTRUCTION BITS				MEANING	
28	29	30	31		
0	0	0	0	No Action	
0	0	0	1	IL	Increment LOC by instruction length
0	0	1	0	PW2	Privileged write halfword (2 bytes)
0	0	1	1	DW2	Data write halfword
0	1	0	0	No Action	
0	1	0	1	I4DW4	Increment MAR by 4, data write fullword
0	1	1	0	PW4	Privileged write fullword
0	1	1	1	DW4	Data write fullword
1	0	0	0	RAS	Read halfword and set sign bit
1	0	0	1	ILIR	Increment LOC by length and read instruction
1	0	1	0	PR2	Privileged read halfword
1	0	1	1	DR2	Data read halfword
1	1	0	0	IR	Instruction read
1	1	0	1	I4DR4	Increment MAR by 4, data read fullword
1	1	1	0	PR4	Privileged read fullword
1	1	1	1	DR4	Data read fullword

Notes:

IL   The location counter (LOC) is incremented by the length in bytes
        of the last user level instruction fetched.

PW2   The memory access controller (MAC) is disabled and the halfword
        in MDR, bits 16:31, is written into the addressed location.

DW2   The halfword in MDR, bits 16:31, is written into the addressed location.
        MAC is not disabled.

I4DW4   The memory address register (MAR) is incremented by four. Then the fullword
        in MDR, bits 0:31, is written into the location addressed by MAR.

PW4   The MAC is disabled and the fullword in MDR, bits 0:31, is written into
        the addressed location.

DW4   The fullword in MDR, bits 0:31, is written into the addressed location.

RAS   The halfword at the addressed location is read then rewritten with bit 0
        of the halfword set. The original value of the halfword replaces MDR
        bits 16:31. Bits 0:15 of the MDR are set equal to bit 16
        of MDR (Sign extension).

ILIR   LOC is incremented by the length in bytes of the last user instruction fetched.
        Then an instruction read is started from the address specified
        by the new value of LOC.

                                                              (Continued)

Table 5-4 (Continued)

PR2   The MAC is disabled and the halfword at the addressed location is read and copied to MDR bits 16:31. Bits 0:15 of MDR are set equal to MDR bit 16.

DR2   The halfword at the addressed location is read and copied to MDR bits 16:31. Bits 0:15 of MDR are set equal to MDR bit 16.

IR   An instruction read is started from the memory address specified by LOC.

I4DR4   MAR is incremented by four. Then the fullword at the location addressed by the new value of MAR is read and copied to MDR.

PR4   MAC is disabled. Then the fullword at the location addressed by MAR is read and copied to MDR.

DR4   The fullword at the location addressed by MAR is read and copied to MDR.

5.3.2 Microinstruction Types

The general nature of each of six types of microinstructions will be explained in the following paragraphs.

Address Link

The incremented contents of the ROM location counter (RLC) are placed in the selected S bus destination register. Then, if the specified test condition is met (true if $T = 1$, false if $T = 0$), transfer takes place and the next microinstruction is taken from the control store location specified in the ADDRESS field. Otherwise, the next microinstruction in sequence is the next to be executed. MC and D operations occur only if the transfer is not made. If $X = 1$, then the ADDRESS field addresses a microinstruction that is executed if the test condition is met, and the next microinstruction in the original sequence is always the next to be executed.

Register Branch

Similar to Address Link except that the address to be branched to is taken from the register on the B bus. If $X = 1$, then the B bus register contains a microinstruction that is executed if the test condition is met, and the next microinstruction in the original sequence is always the next to be executed.

Register to Register Transfer

Performs operation F using A and B register operands and places the results in S register. Also provides for conditional transfer if C is 1; in this case a limited range transfer is performed by replacing the six low order RLC bits with the PAGE ADDRESS.

Register to Register Control

Performs operation F-K using A and B register operands and places the results in S register. Specified MC or D operations occur *after* the basic register to register function has completed execution (as is true for all microinstructions with MC and D options).

Register to Register Immediate

Performs operation F using A register operand and DATA field (plus leading 0's or 1's, depending on bit 20 of the DATA field) and places the results in S register. (If I = 1, DATA contains address in control store of the actual second operand.)

Register Write

Stores the contents of A register in the control store location whose address is contained in the B register.

5.3.3 Microinstruction Sequencing

Model 8/32 microinstructions are normally executed sequentially using addresses from the incrementing RLC register. Address Link and Register Branch type microinstructions provide for unlimited range conditional transfers, while register to register transfers allow conditional transfers within a 64-location range in control store.

Link options and register set flexibility can support both nested subroutines and block structured microprogramming. Careful manipulation of the active register set designation field along with the remainder of the PSW could conceivably support up to eight distinct levels.

5.4 INTERRUPTS

With the standard Model 8/32, all interrupts should be considered as *hard* in that they generally cause automatic transfers to microprogram locations within the first five pages of control store, which include the fixed ROM emulator of the user level 8/32 machine. The privileged/illegal user instruction interrupt, memory access controller, machine malfunction, and primary power fail interrupts are all generated internally by the hardware. Additional internal interrupts such as arithmetic faults, queue service, and supervisor calls originate within the emulator and are handled therein as well.

External interrupts are hardware driven and include both a console interrupt and four priority interrupts to be associated with peripheral devices (see section 5.5, I/O). External interrupts remain active until recognized and serviced by the processor.

As noted in Table 5-1, machine malfunction and memory access controller (relocation/protection) interrupts may be individually enabled/disabled by bits (18 and 21) within the PSW. In addition, bits 17 and 20 enable or disable external interrupts on the basis of levels, where the current level is determined by the designated active register set. Microinstructions are also available in the Branch/Execute and Link set that can collectively enable or disable all interrupts except those of the memory access controller.

The interrupt system is further tied to the emulator in that the preferred time for handling interrupts is between user level instructions. The display console interrupt, for example, is tested only during the Decode (D) option of a microinstruction. True general purpose microprogramming or emulation of another machine avoiding 8/32 hardware assist features will therefore be complicated by the standard interrupt system.

5.5 INPUT/OUTPUT

The Model 8/32 input/output system employs the 33-line D bus (or multiplexor bus). Line assignments are indicated in Table 5-5. All I/O operations are either halfword (16-bit) or byte (8-bit) oriented. Since all 16 data lines are always used, special *byte steering* hardware is employed to handle byte transfers. Any time a halfword oriented device is being utilized, the halfword (HW) line becomes active and suppresses the byte steering hardware.

A large number of microinstructions are available to facilitate I/O operations. They utilize the basic formats previously discussed, speci-

Table 5-5: D Bus (Multiplexor) Lines (Courtesy Interdata Inc.).

LINE		DIRECTION	
Function	Mnem	Processor	Device
Data Lines:	D00	←——————→	
	D01	←——————→	
	.	.	
	.	.	
	.	.	
	D15	←——————→	
Control Lines:			
Status Request	SR	——————→	
Data Request	DR	——————→	
I/O Command	CMD	——————→	
Data Available	DA	——————→	
Address	ADRS	——————→	
Acknowledge	ACK0	——————→	
	ACK1	——————→	
	ACK2	——————→	
	ACK3	——————→	
Control Line	CL07	——————→	
Test Lines:			
Attention	ATN0	←——————	
	ATN1	←——————	
	ATN2	←——————	
	ATN3	←——————	
Synchronize	SYN	←——————	
Halfword	HW	←——————	
Initialize	SCLR	——————→	

fying module 2, the I/O module. The repertoire provides for acknowledging interrupts, addressing devices, sensing device status, issuing I/O commands, and reading or writing data (both bytes and halfwords). Addresses are normally placed in an A source register and commands in a B source register. Status and device number information from peripherals are passed to the processor via the indicated S destination register.

Bidirectional data lines are used to pass commands, data, addresses, and status. Devices signal the processor using one of the priority interrupt attention lines. The processor in turn (by micro-instruction) acknowledges requests for attention using acknowledge lines. Additional communication occurs in the form of special 8-bit commands, data or status requests or data available signals from the processor. Device controllers respond to these signals using the syn-chronize (SYN) line.

Input/output operations are fully asynchronous. Microinstructions may result in one, two, or three operations occurring on the D bus, each lasting until a SYN is received from the device.

5.6 ORGANIZATIONAL PARAMETERS

Basic machine cycle time for the Model 8/32 is 240 nanoseconds; most microinstructions execute in that time. Those microinstructions that require an additional fetch of data from the control store (for example, I = 1 for indirect B operand) execute in 360 nanoseconds, the additional 120 nanoseconds reflecting the control store access time. Cycle time for the core main memory is 750 nanoseconds.

Chapter 6

Burroughs B1700 Architecture

6.0 SUMMARY DESCRIPTION

The B1700 is a general purpose microprogrammable computer designed to support a variety of intermediate languages (S-machines). Nominal data width is 24 bits; however, masking and iterative techniques readily facilitate support of arbitrary data widths. Memory is addressable down to individual bits to further support variable word lengths.

Four general purpose registers (X, Y, L, T) are available. These are supplemented by a *scratchpad* containing 32 words of 24 bits each, addressable also as 16 words of 48 bits each to handle *data descriptors*. The L and T registers have limited processing capabilities including shifting and extraction functions, and may also be addressed/accessed in 4-bit increments. Major processing facilities include a 24-bit function box and a 4-bit function box. The 24-bit function box may operate on less than 24-bit operands and in binary, BCD, or EBCDIC modes.

Microinstructions are 16 bits long and are vertical in structure. The repertoire includes 32 basic microinstructions with a wide range of variants. Microprograms may be executed from main memory or from control store; from 1 to 4K words of read-write control store may be provided depending on the processor model. Microinstructions normally execute sequentially with explicit branches to alter the sequence. An address stack is available to support microsubroutines. Dynamic microprogramming is possible on the B1700.

91

6.1 INTRODUCTION

Burroughs B1700 embodies a unique design tenet: The work done to accomodate definable machine structure from instruction to instruction is less than the work wasted from instruction to instruction when one machine structure is used for all applications. In other words, execution of machine language using procrustean hardware causes more inefficiencies than soft interpretation of arbitrary machine language on protean hardware.[1]

The above quotation summarizes the philosophy employed in the B1700 system. It is one of a relatively small class of machines designed without a machine language (macro) level architecture in mind. Rather, it is intended that the microprogrammable architecture of the B1700 be capable of supporting virtually any intermediate language, not solely for the purpose of emulating other machines, but more generally for the purpose of providing the optimum intermediate language suited to the ultimate task to be performed.

Burroughs refers to these intermediate languages as *S-languages* (S for secondary). The S-language optimized for COBOL execution, for instance, is quite different from that which would be optimum for an operating system. Through dynamic microprogramming, the B1700 can execute different microprogrammed interpreters according to the requirements of the job at hand.

Many of the capabilities of the B1700 (virtual memory, multiprogramming, and so on) are provided by the MCP (master control program), a software package written in a unique, higher level language which is itself interpreted. This chapter will concentrate on the actual physical architecture and will only mention the software provided facilities as they relate to the hardware.

6.2 SYSTEM LEVEL ARCHITECTURE

B1700 systems are available in two system series, B1710 and B1720. The key difference between the two lies in the processor; the

---

[1] Wayne T. Wilner of the Burroughs Corporation in "Design of the B1700," presented at the 1972 FJCC (see WILN72, bibliography.)

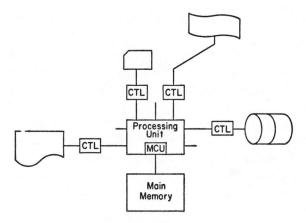

a. B1712 / B1714 Systems Configuration

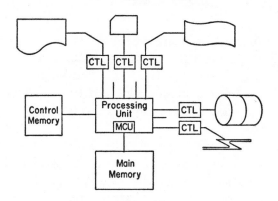

b. B1726 System Configuration

Fig. 6-1: B1700 Series System Configurations
(Courtesy of Burroughs Corp. [BURR72]).

B1710 processor is employed in the B1712/1714 systems, while the B1720 processor is used in the B1726/1728 systems.[2] The architectures of both processors are similar and both are described in the sections that follow, with their differences identified.

System configurations for the two series are illustrated in Figure 6-1a and b. In either case from one to eight I/O channels/controllers

---

[2]B1726 and B1728 systems differ only in the maximum size of memory available (see 6.3.3 and 6.3.4). In all other respects what is said about the B1726 applies also to the B1728 unless specifically stated otherwise.

may be connected to the CPU. MCU refers to the memory control unit which is part of the processor and handles all memory access requests. On the B1710, the memory control unit is connected directly to the processor, while on the B1726 a *port interchange* (8 ports maximum) provides the access path between the processor and memory.

Only the B1726 has a separate, high speed control memory. Microprograms for the B1710 must reside in main memory, while the B1726 may use control memory and/or main memory for microprogram storage. The only difference is in speed, since control memory is approximately four times faster than main memory.

6.3 B1710 AND B1726 PROCESSORS

The B1700 processor architecture (Figure 6-2) includes two major arithmetic/logic processing units, a 24-bit function box and a 4-bit function box, as well as a number of working registers which themselves have a limited processing (shift/rotate, extract) capability. A large bank of scratchpad registers is also available for general purpose use.

Nominal data width within the B1700 is 24 bits. The microprogrammer has available control facilities that enable him to process any bit length from 1 to 24 bits, and, through iterative techniques, to any length beyond 24 as well. This variable data length capability is also supported by the main memory which is addressable down to individual bits and effectively up to any desired field length.

The architecture is largely oriented around the registers, most of which are capable of serving as both a source and destination. *Pseudoregisters* are also available that provide (source only) access to data as if they were available in actual physical registers; all outputs of the 24-bit function box are addressable in this manner. Microinstructions generally call for a single source and/or a single destination register.

6.3.1 Processing Facilities

Twenty-four-Bit Function Box

A functional representation of the 24-bit function box is shown in Figure 6-3. Data inputs are from the X and Y registers and the carry

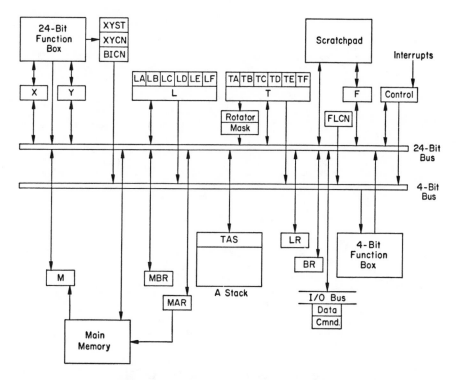

Fig. 6-2: B1712 Simplified Block Diagram.

flip-flop (CYF). Control inputs are the 2-bit CPU register that specifies the arithmetic unit type, and the 5-bit CPL register that specifies the actual length of the operands. CPU codes provide for arithmetic unit types of 1-bit (binary) operands, 4-bit (binary coded decimal) operands, or 8-bit (EBCDIC) operands, with the EBCDIC capability restricted to the B1726 version. Operand lengths as indicated by CPL must be an integer multiple of the unit type (n X 1, n X 4, n X 8) for correct results.

A unique feature of the B1700 is the apparent simultaneous availability of all the arithmetic and logic functions of X and Y in a set of output pseudoregisters. The nine outputs and their pseudo-register names are as shown in Figure 6-3. The microprogrammer need only load X and Y with the desired operands (assuming CYF, CPU, and CPL have previously been set), and all nine functions will be immediately generated and available in their respective registers; changing any input immediately changes all outputs.

In addition to the usual arithmetic and logic functions of two

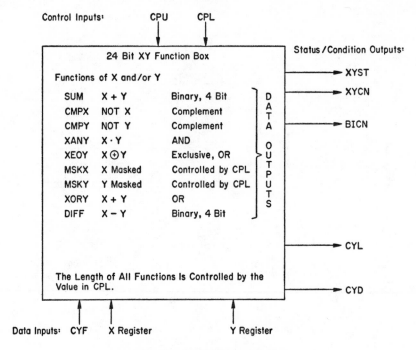

Fig. 6-3: 24-Bit Function Box
(Courtesy of Burroughs Corp [BURR72]).

variables, MSKX and MSKY result registers are filled with the low order number of bits specified by CPL from X and Y respectively, while the high order remaining bit positions are filled with leading zeroes. Status and condition results are also produced and placed in 4-bit pseudoregisters as shown in Figure 6-4. CYF can be set using the SET CYF microinstruction.

Four-Bit Function Box

Unlike its 24-bit counterpart, the 4-bit function box operates in a more traditional manner with specified source and destination registers and a single functional operation called for (see 4-Bit Manipulate Microinstruction, Figure 6-8). Besides the 4-bit status, condition and control registers, a number of working registers are addressable in 4-bit increments as will be seen; generally, any of these 4-bit registers may be a source and any that are not pseudoregisters may be a destination.

a. X/Y State (XYST) Register:

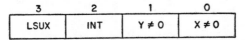

3	2	1	0
LSUX	INT	Y ≠ O	X ≠ O

LSUX = Least significant unit of X. (True if least significant unit of
X = 1 in binary mode (CPU = OO), = 1001 in 4-bit mode (CPU = 01),
and undefined for other CPU values.)

INT   = Interrupt.

b. X/Y Condition (XYCN) Register:

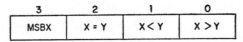

3	2	1	0
MSBX	X = Y	X < Y	X > Y

MSBX = Most significant bit of X. (As designated by CPL.)

c. Binary Conditions (BICN) Register:

3	2	1	0
LSUY	CYF	CYD	CYL

CYL   = Carry out level.
CYD   = Borrow out level.
CYF   = Carry flag.
LSUY = Least significant unit of Y. (See LSUX above.)

Fig. 6-4: Status and Condition Pseudo Register Outputs of the
24-Bit Function Box.

One input comes from a specified source register and the second input is included as a literal field in the microinstruction. Results are returned to the source register (except pseudoregisters).

Available functions include SET, AND, OR, Exclusive-OR, SUM (Modulo 16), and DIFFERENCE (Modulo 16). Sum and difference functions may also provide for skipping the next microinstruction if a carry (borrow) is produced.

Shift/Rotate/Extract

Shifts, rotations, and data extractions are not accomplished by dedicated processing units, but rather are special capabilities of key working registers as described in the following section.

6.3.2 Local Store

General Purpose Registers

The X and Y general purpose working registers have already been mentioned as the operand inputs to the 24-bit function box. Additionally, they have the capability of shifting or rotating their contents either individually or together as a concatenated 48-bit register. (Rotating X and Y is possible only with the B1726.) Addressable as either source or destination registers, the X and Y registers are also capable of read-write operations with main memory.

Two additional general purpose 24-bit registers are the L and T registers. Like X and Y, they are both capable of main memory read-write operations. The T register has shift/rotate capabilities, and, further, is the one register from which a 1–24 bit length field can be extracted beginning with any bit position; this is a particularly useful operation for target instruction decoding in emulation.

In addition to their roles as full 24-bit registers, L and T are addressable in 4-bit increments as subregisters (Figure 6-5). This allows for testing and/or altering any of the 4-bit groups of these registers using the 4-bit function box or testing/branching microinstructions.

Scratchpad

A scratchpad of 16 registers (S00–S15) each 48 bits in length is available for the primary purpose of holding field descriptors of operands (see Figure 6-7 and the discussion of main memory in section 6.3.3). Alternatively, these registers may be addressed as 32 registers (S00A–S15A, S00B–S15B) each 24 bits in length, and they may also be used as general purpose registers. In contrast to other registers that can be addressed and used as sources/destinations in many microinstructions, scratchpad registers can only be accessed through a few dedicated scratchpad microinstructions.

Control Register

The 24-bit control register (C) is actually a collection of independent subregisters as indicated in Figure 6-6. The functions of CPL, CPU, and CYF were discussed along with the 24-bit function box. Only 1 bit (3) of CD is actually used and its function is to indicate a memory parity error. CC is used for four other possible interrupt

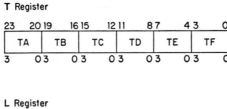

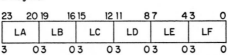

Fig. 6-5: Four-Bit Subregister Addressability of the T and L Registers.

conditions, console interrupt, I/O service request, timer interrupt (set automatically by the hardware every 100 milliseconds), and console state.

The 4-bit CA and CB fields are general purpose registers available for use as desired by the microprogrammer. Addressable as both sources and destinations, they may be set, manipulated, and tested just as other 4-bit registers and can be particularly useful in emulation for keeping track of target machine status.

6.3.3 Main Memory and Memory Control

It has already been pointed out that the B1700 does not have a fixed word size, but rather operates on defined fields, whose lengths may vary from as small as a single bit. In support of this concept, memory is addressable down to the individual bit.

Available memory sizes are from 16K bytes minimum (B1712) to 256K bytes maximum (B1728).[3] Although physical memory is byte oriented, special hardware (*field isolation units*) is used to achieve bit addressability and variable lengths crossing normal byte boundaries. In effect, then, memory sizes of 128K bits minimum to 2M bits are realizable with currently available configurations.

A maximum of 24 bits of data may be handled in a single memory read or write operation. For longer length fields additional read-write microinstruction executions are required.

---

[3] Maximum memory size for the B1726 is 98K bytes.

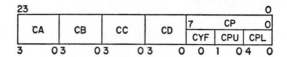

Fig. 6-6: Control Register.

Addressing

Main memory is addressed by a 24-bit absolute address, a 1-bit field direction indicator, and a 5-bit field length value. The absolute address is obtained from the 48-bit definition (F) register (shown in Figure 6-7a), FA field, while the field length and direction are contained in the microinstruction. The field length contained in the FL field of the F register describes the actual total length of the data field (up to 65K bits) which may require multiple 24-bit memory accesses to handle. FU and FT specify units of data (binary, 4-bit binary, and so on) and type, and do not affect memory operation. Microinstructions are available (B1726 only) to move descriptors between 48-bit scratchpad registers and the F register.

The field length condition register (FLCN) is a 4-bit register that continuously indicates the results of a comparison between FL and the similar field of the descriptor stored in scratchpad S00B; used in conjunction with the capability to increment or decrement FL in the memory read-write microinstruction, the FLCN register can facilitate control of multiple read-write operations in handling fields greater than 24-bits in length.

Memory base and limit registers (BR, LR) are available as source and destination registers. They allow the microprogrammer to implement base relative addressing and memory protection (without sacrificing other general purpose registers), as is done in the MCP.

6.3.4 Control Store

A single level of logical control store is utilized in the B1700 architecture. Only the B1726 has a physically separate control store, while the B1710 stores its microprograms in main memory.

Control memory sizes of 1K or 2K words are available for the B1726, with 3K and 4K sizes also available for the B1728. Like the

a.

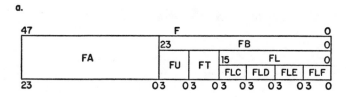

b.

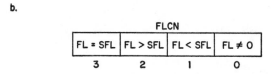

Fig. 6-7: Field Definition (F) and Field Length Condition (FLCN) Registers.

B1710, the B1726 can also execute microprograms from main memory and hence the 2K maximum physical size is not a limiting factor. Word size in control memory is 16 bits, the length of a single microinstruction.

An *Overlay* microinstruction provides the capability of writing a variable number of microinstructions into the read-write control memory from main memory. The FA, FL, and L registers are used to hold the necessary parameters.

A group of three key registers are used by the B1726 to permit fetching microinstructions from either control memory or main memory. The A register contains the logical address of the next microinstruction; the top of control memory (TOPM) indicates the number of K bytes of control memory in the system; and the memory base register (MBR) points to the base location in main memory at which microprograms are stored. Internal logic compares the contents of A and TOPM X 512 to determine if the next address lies within physical control memory; if not, the microinstruction is fetched from main memory location (A X 16) + MBR. The B1710 has only the A register.

Additional facilities used with control memory will be discussed in the following section on microinstruction sequencing.

6.3.5 Microinstructions and Processor Control

General

Microinstructions for the B1700 are 16 bits in length and may be considered vertical. The multiplicity of highly encoded formats is shown in Table 6-1, along with the possible values of most of the *variants* called for that are shown in Table 6-2.[4] Source and destination registers are addressed via a row and column matrix with 4-bit registers grouped in columns 0 and 1 (Table 6-2).

The microinstruction currently being executed is held in the 16-bit M register which is itself capable of being accessed as a source or destination register. Since M is loaded by ORing with the present contents, a MOVE to M may be used to modify the *next* microinstruction without altering it in memory.

It is interesting to note the opcode scheme employed within the microinstructions. As can be seen in Table 6-1, from 4 to 16 bits may be used for the variable length opcode field; within the constraints of bits required for necessary variants, shorter length opcodes are generally used for more frequently executed microinstructions, and longer opcodes for less frequently executed microinstructions. A constant length opcode field would have required at least one additional bit in every microinstruction, since 5 bits would be required for the opcode field (32 microinstructions) and many only require 4 bits with this scheme.

Microinstruction Sequencing

Execution of microinstructions is normally from sequential locations in control (or main) memory, with explicit branches forced by conditional or unconditional branching microinstructions. A 12-bit dedicated high speed adder facilitates incrementing the A register for relative branches.

An address stack of 32 words (16 in the B1710) each 24 bits long is used to hold microinstruction addresses in a last in, first out (LIFO) mode; the 24-bit length permits operand storage as well. This

---

[4] Although not all commands shown are available for the B1710 system, Burroughs software provides for B1710-B1720 compatibility by automatically generating B1710 microinstruction sequences equivalent to "not available" microinstructions.

Table 6-1: B1700 Microinstructions and Formats (Courtesy of Burroughs Corp. [Burr72]).

Micromnemonics	OP CODE HEXADECIMAL	15 14 13 12	11 10 9 8	7 6	5 4	3 2 1 0
Register Move	1nnn	0 0 0 1	SOURCE REG ROW	SOURCE REG COL	DESTINATION REG COL	DESTINATION REG ROW
Scratchpad Move	2nnn	0 0 1 0	SOURCE DESTINATION REG ROW	SOURCE DEST REG COL	REG TO SP / SP TO REG A / B	SCRATCHPAD WORD ADDRESS
Four bit Manipulate	3nnn	0 0 1 1	AFFECTED REGISTER ROW	REG COL	MANIPULATE VARIANTS	FOUR BIT MANIPULATE LITERAL
Bit Test Rel Br on False	4nnn	0 1 0 0	SOURCE REG (FOUR BIT) ROW	REG COL	TEST BIT NUMBER + / –	RELATIVE BRANCH DISPLACEMENT VALUE
Bit Test Rel Br on True	5nnn	0 1 0 1	SOURCE REG (FOUR BIT) ROW	REG COL	TEST BIT NUMBER + / –	RELATIVE BRANCH DISPLACEMENT VALUE
Skip When	6nnn	0 1 1 0	SOURCE REG (FOUR BIT) ROW	REG COL	SKIP TEST VARIANTS	FOUR BIT TEST MASK
Read/Write Memory	7nnn	0 1 1 1	R / W COUNT FA/FL VARIANTS	DATA REG (XYTL)	FOR / REV	MEMORY FIELD LENGTH
Move Eight Bit Literal	8nnn	1 0 0 0	DESTINATION REG ROW COL 2 ASSUMED	EIGHT-BIT LITERAL		

M REGISTER

(Continued)

Table 6-1: B1700 Microinstructions and Formats (Continued)

Micromnemonics	OP CODE HEXADECIMAL	15	14	13	12	11	10	9	8	7	6	5	4	3	2	1	0
							M REGISTER										
Move 24-Bit Literal	9nnn	1	0	0	1	DESTINATION REG ROW COL 2 ASSUMED				FIRST EIGHT BITS OF LITERAL							
Shift/Rotate T Register	Annn	1	0	1	0	DESTINATION REG ROW				DEST REG COL		SFT / ROT	SHIFT ROTATE COUNT (1-24)				
Extract from T Register	Bnnn	1	0	1	1	RIGHT BIT POINTER (1-24) FOR EXTRACTION FIELD OP				DEST REG CODE (XYTL)		WIDTH OF EXTRACTION FIELD (1-24)					
Branch Rel Forward	Cnnn	1	1	0	0	RELATIVE DISPLACEMENT MAGNITUDE											
Branch Rel Reverse	Dnnn	1	1	0	1	RELATIVE DISPLACEMENT MAGNITUDE											
Call Rel Forward	Ennn	1	1	1	0	RELATIVE CALLED ADDRESS MAGNITUDE											
Call Rel Reverse	Fnnn	1	1	1	1	RELATIVE CALLED ADDRESS MAGNITUDE											
Swap Memory	02nn	0	0	0	0	0	0	1	0	DEST GEN PURPOSE REG (XYTL)		FOR / REV	MEMORY FIELD LENGTH				
Clear Registers*	03nn	0	0	0	0	0	0	1	1	L REG	T REG	Y REG	X REG	FA REG	FL REG	FU REG	CP REG

Instruction	Code	Bit Pattern	Variant Field	Field
Shift/Rotate X or Y	04nn	0 0 0 0 0 1 0 0	SFT/ROT · LFT/RT · X/Y	SHIFT ROTATE COUNT (1-24)
Shift/Rotate X and Y	05nn	0 0 0 0 0 1 0 1	SFT/ROT* · LFT/RT · RES	SHIFT ROTATE COUNT (1-24)
Count FA and FL	06nn	0 0 0 0 0 1 1 0	COUNT VARIANTS	LITERAL MAGNITUDE
Exchange Doublepad Word	07nn	0 0 0 0 0 1 1 1	DESTINATION 48-BIT SCRATCHPAD ADDR	SOURCE 48-BIT SCRATCHPAD ADDR
Scratchpad Relate FA	08nn	0 0 0 0 1 0 0 0	RESERVED (+ / −)	A(LEFT) SCRATCHPAD WORD ADDRESS
Monitor	09nn	0 0 0 0 1 0 0 1	LITERAL OCCURRENCE IDENTIFIER	
Cassette Control	002n	0 0 0 0 0 0 1 0	CASSETTE MANIPULATE VARIANTS	RES
Bias	003n	0 0 0 0 0 0 1 1	BIAS VARIANTS	TEST / NO / TEST
Store F into Doublepad Word*	004n	0 0 0 0 0 1 0 0	DESTINATION SCRATCHPAD WORD (48 BITS)	

(Continued)

Table 6-1: B1700 Microinstructions and Formats (Continued)

Micromnemonics	OP CODE HEXADECIMAL	15 14 13 12	11	10	9	8	7	6	5	4	3	2	1	0
Load F from Doublepad Word*	005n	0 0 0 0	0	0	0	0	0	1	0	1	SOURCE SCRATCHPAD WORD (48 BITS)			
Set CYF	006n	0 0 0 0	0	0	0	0	0	1	0	1	CYF TO CYD	CYF TO CYL	CYF TO 1	CYF TO 0
Halt	0001	0 0 0 0	0	0	0	0	0	0	0	0	0	0	0	1
Overlay M String*	0002	0 0 0 0	0	0	0	0	0	0	0	0	0	0	1	0
Normalize X	0003	0 0 0 0	0	0	0	0	0	0	0	0	0	0	1	1
No Operation	0000	0 0 0 0	0	0	0	0	0	0	0	0	0	0	0	0

M REGISTER

ONE BIT VARIANT 0 / 1

*Not available on B1710 systems

Table 6-2: Microinstruction Variant Codes (Courtesy Burroughs Corp. [BURR72]).

FOUR-BIT MANIPULATE
(3nnn) VARIANTS

BITS 4-6	CONDITIONS
000	SET
001	AND
010	OR
011	EOR
100	INC
101	INC/TEST
110	DEC
111	DEC/TEST

EXTRACT FROM T REGISTER
(8nnn) VARIANTS

BITS 5-6	CONDITIONS
00	X REG.
01	Y REG.
10	T REG.
11	L REG.

COUNT FA AND FL
(06nn) VARIANTS

BITS 5-7	CONDITIONS
000	NOP
001	FA↑
010	FL↑
011	FA↑ FL↓
100	FA↓ FL↑
101	FA↓
110	FL↓
111	FA↓ FL↓

SKIP WHEN (6nnn) SKIP
TEST VARIANTS

BITS 4-6	CONDITIONS
000	ANY SKIP
001	ALL SKIP
010	EQU SKIP
011	ALL CLR SKIP
100	NOT ANY SKIP
101	NOT ALL SKIP
110	NOT EQU SKIP
111	NOT ALL CLR SKIP

(Continued)

Table 6-2: Microinstruction Variant Codes (Continued)

SWAP MEMORY (02nn) VARIANTS	
BITS 6-7	**CONDITIONS**
00	X REG.
01	Y REG.
10	T REG.
11	L REG.

DISPATCH (001n) VARIANTS	
BITS 1-3	**CONDITIONS**
000	DISPATCH LOCK
001	DISPATCH WRITE
010	DISPATCH READ
011	DISPATCH RD & CLR
100	RESERVED
101	RESERVED
110	RESERVED
111	RESERVED

READ/WRITE MEMORY (7nnn) VARIANTS	
BITS 6-7	**CONDITIONS**
00	X REG.
01	Y REG.
10	T REG.
11	L REG.
BITS 8-10	**CONDITIONS**
000	NOP
001	FA$\uparrow$
010	FL$\uparrow$
011	FA$\uparrow$ FL$\downarrow$
100	FA$\downarrow$ FL$\uparrow$
101	FA$\downarrow$
110	FL$\downarrow$
111	FA$\downarrow$ FL$\downarrow$

(Continued)

Table 6-2: Microinstruction Variant Codes (Continued)

CASSETTE CONTROL (002n) VARIANTS

BITS 3-1	CONDITIONS
000	START TAPE
001	STOP ON GAP
010	STOP ON X≠Y
011-111	RESERVED

BIAS (003n) VARIANTS

BITS 3-1	CONDITIONS
000	FU
001	24 OR FL
010	24 OR SFL
011	24 OR FL OR SFL
100	NOP
101	24 OR CPL OR FL
110	NOP
111	24 OR CPL OR FL OR SFL

REGISTER COLUMN

CC REGISTER
0 = CONSOLE INTR.
1 = I/O SERVICE REQ.
2 = CLOCK INTR (100 MS)
3 = STATE FLAG

CD REGISTER
0 = WRT/SWAP OUT OF BDS*
1 = READ OUT OF BDS*
2 = OUT OF BDS OVERRIDE*
3 = MEM. RD. PARITY ERR.

INCN REGISTER*
0 = PORT DISP. LOCKOUT
1 = PORT DISP. INTR.
2 = PORT PRIORITY INTR.
3 = MISSING CONTROLLER ON PORT
    OR CHANNEL

REGISTER ROW

	0	1	2	3
0	TA	FU	X	SUM
1	TB	FT	Y	CMPX
2	TC	FLC	T	CMPY
3	TD	FLD	L	XANY
4	TE	FLE	A(MAR)	XEOY
5	TF	FLF	M	MSKX
6	CA	BICN	BR	MSKY
7	CB	FLCN	LR	XORY
8	LA	TOPM*	FA	DIFF
9	LB	RES.	FB	MAXS
10	LC	RES.	FL	MAXM
11	LD	RES.	TAS	U
12	LE	XYCN	CP	MBR*
13	LF	XYST	MSMA*	DATA
14	CC	INCN*	READ	CMND
15	CD	CPU	WRIT	NULL

*NOT AVAILABLE ON B1710 SYSTEMS

facility provides a powerful microsubroutine capability. It is accessed by MOVEs to the top of the A stack (TAS) register, or CALLs, or MOVEs from the TAS; these microinstructions push and pop the stack to save and recall addresses or operands as desired.

Interrupts

All interrupts within the B1700 processors are soft in that they must be explicitly tested for and reacted to by microinstructions. The CC and CD fields of the control register (plus a B1726 interrupt conditions [INCN] register) provide indicators for interrupts that can be tested for, with conditional branches to interrupt handling microroutines.

6.4 INPUT/OUTPUT

Input/output operations in B1700 systems are handled by I/O controllers after being initiated by the processor. A 24-bit DATA pseudoregister serves as an I/O buffer register; data are passed to and from the I/O controller using MOVEs to and from the DATA register. Similarly, I/O commands are passed to the I/O controller using the CMND register.

A tape cassette is available for specialized input, normally of microinstructions. TAPE mode selectable by console switch permits the processor to accept and execute microinstructions directly from the cassette unit. Data input from the cassette are available to the processor in the 16-bit U register, accessable as a source for MOVE operations only.

6.5 ORGANIZATIONAL PARAMETERS

Basic clock rates in the B1712, B1714, and B1726 processors are 2MHz, 4MHz, and 6HMz respectively. Read-write cycle times of the three processors are thus 2-3 microseconds (B1712), 1-1.5 micro-seconds (B1714), and 667-1000 nanoseconds (B1726) respectively, based on four clocks for a read cycle and six clocks for a write cycle.

6.6 SUMMARY

The B1700 architecture is particularly well suited to general purpose microprogramming. The processing facilities and microinstruction repertoire give the microprogrammer the capability of coding efficient emulators, functionally oriented intermediate (S) languages, or directly executed application programs. Finally, the defined field concept together with the bit addressable main memory not only facilitate handling of variable data lengths, but, in addition, serve to maximize the efficient use of available memory.

Chapter 7

Nanodata QM-1 Architecture

7.0 SUMMARY DESCRIPTION

The Nanodata QM-1 is a general purpose computer employing two levels of control below the traditional machine language (macro) level. The micro level machine with microprograms residing in control store is not completely defined; the lower *nano* level machine which executes *nanoprograms* from *nano store* will define the micro level machine in the same manner in which a micro level program defines a macro level machine.

The QM-1 nano level machine is a horizontally structured machine that exercises detailed control over the hardware. Control is divided between nanoinstructions (a 72-bit K vector and 72-bit T vector, or 144 bits total) and a set of residual control F registers (F store).

Data words may be either 16 or 18 bits in length. An ALU and shifter operate in either of the two modes, and also support a decimal mode. Local store consists of a bank of 32 general purpose registers, some of which also perform special purpose functions. A prime function of the residual control F registers is to control the buses providing interconnection between the major functional units and the local store registers; for example, three F registers select two local store registers to supply left and right ALU inputs and a third to receive the ALU output.

The 144-bit nanoinstruction includes over 60 fields. Individual fields control selections of input/output sources/destinations, specifications of control variables, and detailed gating of register/functional unit contents and initiation of actions. The nanoinstructions also control the setting of the residual F store contents. The nanoprogrammer must have a thorough understanding of hardware functions and timing constraints.

112

Nano store is writable and may contain up to 1K "words," each word consisting of a single K vector and four associated T vectors for a total of 360 bits. T vectors are selected sequentially while the K vector is held constant. Explicit branches with a variety of possible test actions select new nanowords. The contents of nano store may be dynamically altered.

7.1 INTRODUCTION

The most unique architecture presented in this book is that of the QM-1 from Nanodata Corporation. It represents the only commercially available machine that employs two true levels of control store, a nano store at what is termed the nanoprogrammable level, and a control store at the microprogrammable level. The potential thus exists for tailoring not only the macro level architecture, but the micro level architecture as well.

At the lowest level, horizontal nanoinstructions exercise near direct control over the hardware. To a large extent the busing interconnections are even programmable. The micro level architecture implemented via nanoprogramming will generally be a vertically organized machine, although only a minimum of constraints are actually imposed.

This chapter will deal primarily with the nano level architecture examining the horizontal control concept and the application of residual control in some detail. At the same time, the features that influence the higher level microprogrammable architecture will become apparent. Because the nano level machine is horizontal in structure, the discussions will of necessity be somewhat detailed.

7.2 QM-1 CPU

Major Units

A system overview block diagram is presented in Figure 7-1. The hardware includes a hierarchy of stores (main store, control store, nano store, plus local store, external store, and F store), functional processing facilities (ALU, shifter, index ALU), and buses that generally connect the stores and processing facilities to the local store.

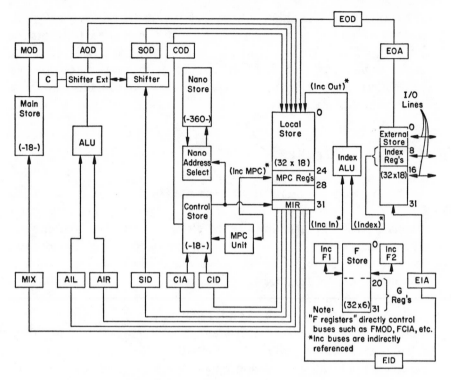

Fig. 7-1: Block Diagram of Nanodata QM-1
(Courtesy of Nanodata Corp.).

Conceptually, it is possible to separate the architecture into an 18-bit data oriented portion (the major stores, ALU, shifter, and associated buses), and a 6-bit residual control portion (the F store and associated facilities), both of which are controlled by the nano-program.

Buses

Three-letter acronyms are used to label the various buses shown in the diagram. The first letter indicates the major unit with which the bus is associated (A = ALU, C = control store, E = external store, M = main store, S = shifter); the second letter defines the direction of data flow (I = input to the unit from local store, O = output from the unit to local store); and the third letter contains further information (A = address, D = data, L = left, R = right, X = multiplex).

Each of twelve buses is connected to a single local store register (at any one time) as selected by the nanoprogrammer and as specified in a residual control register. Two additional buses provide connection between two of the local store buses and external store (EIA, EOA). A bus may connect to only one register, but more than one bus may connect to a single register (producing the logical OR of the bus inputs as the register contents). Since all the buses are independent, it is theoretically possible for the nanoprogrammer to cause up to 12 data transfers to occur simultaneously.

Control

Control exercised by the nanoprogrammer is very close to the hardware level. Six-bit registers in the F store are used to contain residual control information, such as bus connections, that change infrequently. Nanoinstructions themselves contain detailed *nanoprimitives* that effect current (as compared to residual) control over the stores and processing facilities; this control is typically in the form of commands to initiate memory reads-writes and gate information between buses and stores.

7.2.1 Processing Facilities

ALU

The principal processing facility of the QM-1 is the arithmetic logic unit (ALU), which can perform 16 functional operations using two operands. In the normal mode, inputs and outputs are full 18-bit words. A 16-bit mode is also available in which the sign is simply extended over the two high order bits. Finally, a "decimal correction word" can be generated to facilitate decimal arithmetic. For handling negative numbers, 2's complement or 1's complement arithmetic may be performed (or even unsigned arithmetic).

Inputs to the ALU are from the arithmetic input left (AIL) bus, the arithmetic input right (AIR) bus, and the carry-in-hold flip-flop. Control information is provided both by the current nanoinstruction (KALC field, Figure 7-2), and by the FIDX (F store) register that permits residual arithmetic unit control over the selection of 16- or 18-bit mode. ALU output is through the shifter extension to the arithmetic output data (AOD) bus, the carry output condition, the use of which is separately controlled by another nanoinstruction

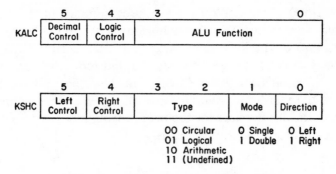

Fig. 7-2: Details of Significant Nanoinstruction Fields.

field (CARRY CTL), and an overflow condition separately testable. A carry-out-hold (COH) flip-flop is available and can be set by the carry output condition, according to CARRY CTL.

The full range of ALU capabilities available can be appreciated through study of Table 7-1, which details outputs produced as a function of the inputs and control functions. Decimal corrections, when produced, are placed on the shifter output data (SOD) bus for subsequent use by the nanoprogrammer.

Shifter

Two shifting modes are available, *single* and *double*. In single mode, only the shifter itself is used and the shifter extension merely passes the ALU output onto the AOD bus; the contents of the shift input data (SID) bus can then be shifted (independent of ALU activities) and the shifted result placed on the SOD bus. Double mode uses the shifter extension as well as the shifter to shift a 36-bit word from the combined ALU output and SID bus.

Control over the shifter is through the KSHC field in the current nanoinstruction (Figure 7-2). The nanoprogrammer can specify direction, mode, and type (circular, logical, arithmetic) of shift and also influences both the source of the low order bit of SOD (left control) and the input to the carry-out-hold flip-flop (right control). The low order bit of SOD may come from either the low order output bit of the shifter or the carry-out-hold (COH) flip-flop, while the input to the carry-out-hold flip-flop may come from the ALU carry output condition, the SH END (37th bit) of the shifter extension, or the low order bit on the SID bus as selected by the nanoinstruction. Shift

Table 7-1: ALU Functions Available (Courtesy Nanodata Corp.).

Bit 3 Thru Bit 0 Of KALC	LOGICAL FUNCTIONS KALC Bit 4 = 1	ARITHMETIC FUNCTIONS KALC Bit 4 = 0		CARRY-OUT BIT is defined as Carry-in bit . . .
		Carry In Hold = 0	Carry In Hold = 1	
0000	NOT L	L − 1	L	OR L
0001	NOT (L AND R)	(L AND R) − 1	L AND R	OR (L AND R)
0010	NOT L OR R	(L AND NOT R) − 1	L AND NOT R	OR (L AND NOT R)
0011	ALL ONES	ALL ONES	ALL ZEROS	OR ZERO
0100	NOT (L OR R)	(L OR NOT R) + L	(L OR NOT R) + L + 1	
0101	NOT R	(L OR NOT R) + (L AND R)	(L OR NOT R) + (L AND R) + 1	
0110	NOT (L XOR R)	L − R − 1	L − R	AND (L OR NOT R)
0111	L OR NOT R	(L OR NOT R)	(L OR NOT R) + 1	
1000	NOT L AND R	(L OR R) + L	(L OR R) + L + 1	
1001	L XOR R	L + R	L + R + 1	
1010	R	(L OR R) + (L AND NOT R)	(L OR R) + (L AND NOT R) + 1	AND (L OR R)
1011	L OR R	L OR R	(L OR R) + 1	
1100	ALL ZEROS	L + L	L + L + 1	
1101	L AND NOT R	L + (L AND R)	L + (L AND R) + 1	
1110	L AND R	L + (L AND NOT R)	L + (L AND NOT R) + 1	
1111	L (PASS LEFT)	L	L + 1	AND L

L = Left Input   R = Right Input

(Arithmetic Functions Interpreted Assuming 2's Complement.)

amount (number of bits) is controlled by the 6-bit KSHA field of the active nanoinstruction.

Index ALU

A special and dedicated ALU, the Index ALU, is available to facilitate rapid indexing and logical/masking operations on the contents of certain registers of local store. The nanoprogrammer specifies either directly or indirectly four parameters: a local store register to provide one input (AUX2 field of current nanoinstruction points to the field that points to LS register); an index operand source (second input) selected from one of 12 index registers in external store, the contents of the MOD or COD buses, or all 1's (AUX3 field in current nanoinstruction points to field that selects one of these sources); a function to be performed by the Index ALU (FSEL2 field in current nanoinstruction either specifies directly or points to the field that in turn specifies the function); and a local store register to receive the Index ALU output (GSPEC field in current nanoinstruction points to field that points to LS register). The fields pointed to for indirect selection are generally other current nanoinstruction fields (KA, KB, KX), fields of the current *micro*instruction (A, B),[1] or specified residual control registers in F store. A large set of arithmetic and logic functions may be performed in the Index ALU making it a valuable general purpose facility in addition to its indexing/addressing role.

Test Conditions

Six *local conditions* are produced within the ALU, shifter, and associated logic. These include CARRY (C), which is the output of COH flip-flop already discussed; SIGN (S), the high order bit of the AOD bus; RESULT (R), indicating the presence of any 1's in an 18 or 36-bit result for testing for absolute zero; OVERFLOW (O), the logical OR of shift overflow and ALU overflow; and SHB and SLB, the high order and low order bits of the SOD bus. The nanoprogrammer can cause the local conditions to be gated into an F store register (FIST) for retention as *global conditions*. Nanoinstruction control fields ALU STATUS ENABLE and SH STATUS ENABLE permit moving the C, S, R, O bits to global status with the

---

[1] See section 7.2.2.

GATE ALU command and the SHB, SLB bits with the GATE SH command respectively.

7.2.2 Local Store

General Registers

There are a total of 32 registers in local store (LS) (R0–R31), each 18 bits long. In addition to their capabilities as general purpose registers, several have special capabilities that are primarily oriented toward use in implementing a micro level architecture.

Microinstruction Register

The last local store register, R31, is dedicated to functioning as a microinstruction register (MIR). Specifically, it enables 6-bit fields (C, A, B from high order end to low order end) to be accessed and used in subsequent control actions. It thus provides an interface link between the 18-bit data structure and the 6-bit control structure. A more detailed discussion of this register is provided in section 7.2.7, on nano store.

Microprogram Counters

Four local store registers (R24–R27) have special capabilities that enable them to serve as microprogram counters (MPC). Residual control register FMPC designates which of the four is currently acting as the MPC. Under nanoprogram control the MPC may be incremented by +1, +2, the contents of the B field of R31 (6 bits, sign extended, 2's complement convention), or the combined contents of the AB fields of R31 (11 bits, sign extended, 2's complement convention). The results of the incrementing may be used to address control store directly (CS ADDR SELECT field of current nanoinstruction) or be gated back into the physical MPC register (INC MPC primitive in current nanoinstruction, using the GSPEC field to specify increment value or source as above).

Index ALU Sources/Destinations

With the exception of the four MPC registers (R24–R27), any of the local store registers may be used as a source of input to the Index ALU or as a destination to receive the Index ALU output. The operation of this facility was described above in section 7.2.1.

7.2.3 External Store

A second bank of 32 registers, collectively referred to as external store (ES), is partitioned into several groups in support of specific functions. Eight *port registers* (E0–E7) provide the external interface capabilities of the QM-1. Possible Index ALU operand sources are E8–E19 as described above in section 7.2.1; eight of these are general purpose, two (a QM-1 option) may serve as base address and field length registers for use with main store, and two contain "program check masks" to control interrupt enables. The remaining twelve (E20–E31) include alternate base address and field length registers (E20–E21)[2], and compacted addresses to be used for responding to interrupts (see section 7.3.4).

Two nanoprimitives are provided to the nanoprogrammer to control external store data transfers. These are GATE ES which gates the EOD bus contents into its designated local store register, and LOAD ES which loads the designated external store register with the contents of the EID bus. Register designations on both ends of these two buses are established through residual control F store registers.

7.2.4 Control Store

QM-1 control store (CS) is implemented in a read-write semiconductor memory, and is addressable in 18-bit words. Up to 16K words of control store may be included in blocks of 1K words each.

As Figure 7-1 indicates, both the control store input address (CIA) bus and microprogram counter (MPC) can be used to select control store addresses for read-write operations. The CIA bus allows general access for data storage and retrieval permitting use of control store for such things as the emulation of target machine registers, tables, and so on. Addresses from the MPC register would, of course, be used for microinstruction fetching. In addition, the control store address may be obtained from the control store output data (COD) bus to facilitate indirect addressing, or from the output of the Index ALU. Address source selection is effected through the CS ADDR SELECT field of the current nanoinstruction.

An available QM-1 option permits the implementation of a virtual

---

[2]Note that these cannot be indexed.

control store with a total address space of 256 pages of 512 words each, mapped to the physical control store of 32 pages of 512 words. Auxiliary hardware provided with this option includes a high speed associative page selector, and a page access control memory for control store read-write protection.

The nanoprogrammer may control the functions of control store through use of the READ CS and WRITE CS nanoprimitives. After the READ operation, the contents of the selected address appear on the COD bus, from where they may be transferred to local store by the GATE CS nanoprimitive.

7.2.5 Main Store

Main store (MS) is available from a minimum of 16K words to a maximum of 256K in 8K increments. Word size is 18 bits, compatible with control store, local store, and external store.

The input bus to main store is called the main store input multiplex (MIX) bus since it is shared between main store addressing and data functions sequentially. Output is via the main store output data (MOD) bus.

Separate MSGO and MSRS nanoprimitives give the nanoprogrammer the flexibility of using either full or split memory cycles, including a read/modify/write capability. In keeping with the detailed hardware level control exercised elsewhere in the machine, tests for MS Busy and MS Data Invalid must be performed, and a GATE MS nanoprimitive must be accomplished at the proper time to read data out of memory.

An available QM-1 option allows the use of E16 and E17 as indexable main store base and field length registers respectively, and also provides write-protection and address-alarm facilities. Also planned is a QM-1 optional RMI (rotate, mask, and index) unit to provide a limited processing capability on data before it is gated into local store.

7.2.6 F Store and Associated Operations

F store consists of 32 control registers, each 6 bits in length. Generally, these registers are utilized for residual control purposes. Although all are 6 bits long, all the bits are not necessarily utilized.

Bus Control F's

Fourteen of the F store registers provide for control of the buses shown in Figure 7-1. The MOD bus, for example, is connected to the local store register indicated by FMOD. Since only 32 local store registers are available, only 5 bits are required to specify connection, with some exceptions. The high order bit is ignored for registers specifying local store destinations (output from buses); for local store sources (input to buses), a 1 in the high order position causes connection to a source of all 1's rather than a local store register. Exceptions are the MIX and MOD buses that can connect to the port registers in external store and hence have more than 32 possible connections to encode: 32–39 indicate port registers E0–E7; 40–64 yield all 1's for MIX sources, while a GATE MS with FMOD contents of 40–64 results in no operation.

Special F's

Six of the F store registers are referred to as *special F's* and their functions will be briefly mentioned. FACT controls auxiliary actions including interrupt enable and disable (see section 7.3.4), control of the main store relative/direct addressing, and parameters for control store options (CS address translation and RMI functions). FUSR also is used with the optional virtual control store hardware to specify user partition numbers. FMPC selects the local store register to operate as the MPC (values 0–4 correspond to R24–R27 respectively). FIDX has several functions as indicated in Figure 7-3. FIST holds global status of conditions as described in section 7.2.1 and as shown in Figure 7-3. Finally, a *phantom* F store register, FIPH, is provided to facilitate direct transfer of information from one auxiliary field to another as will be described below.

G Registers

The last twelve registers in F store are the G's, G0–G11. These are general purpose 6-bit registers that can be used for constant, scratchpad, temporary storage, or back-up to the other F store registers. In the latter role they add further depth to the concept of residual control and provide the nanoprogrammer with the means to readily change the structure of the machine, and subsequently return it to its original state.

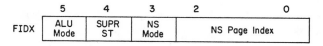

ALU Mode: 0 = 18 bit, 1 = 16 bit
SUPR ST: 1 allows entry to protected nanoprograms
NS Mode: 0 = read-write, 1 = read only

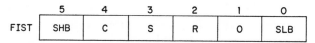

Fig. 7-3: Key F Store Formats.

F Register Operations and the Auxiliary Fields

Transfer of information to and from registers in F store is normally accomplished using the *auxiliary* (AUX) fields, a collection of fields in other registers that can function as sources for transfer into F or destinations for transfer out of F. These include the C, A, and B fields of the MIR (R31), the K fields (KA, KB, KS, KX, KT, KSHA, KSHC, KALC as shown in Table 7-2) of the current nanoinstruction, and other miscellaneous sources. Of particular importance is the fact that the G's may also be used as AUX fields (as sources only) for transfers into F; this allows the G fields to be used for holding information that subsequently can be transferred directly into an F register. Similarly, the use of the phantom F register, FIPH, as a simultaneous source and destination for two AUX transfers results in direct transfer of information from the source AUX to the destination AUX.

Several transfers between AUX fields and F registers can be initiated in a single active nanoinstruction. AUX fields to be used are selected using nanoinstruction fields AUX0, AUX1, AUX2, and AUX3. F store registers to be used are selected using the FSEL0, FSEL1, and FSEL2 fields. Nanoprimitives IN0, IN1, and IN2 can then be used to cause transfers from AUX registers selected by AUX0, AUX1, AUX2 to F registers selected by FSEL0, FSEL1, and FSEL2 respectively. Similarly, nanoprimitives OUT1, OUT2, and OUT3 can command transfers from F registers selected by FSEL0, FSEL1, and FSEL2 to AUX registers selected by AUX0, AUX1, and AUX3 respectively. G's are specified indirectly by reference to the

GSPEC field that points to the desired G. Within the constraints of F and AUX selections, it is theoretically possible to have up to six transfers take place simultaneously.

F register contents can be directly processed in one of two ways. Increment and decrement capabilities exist and are invoked by selection of INCF or DECF as the AUX source in an IN1 and/or IN2 operation. Also, a QM-1 optional 6-bit ALU (the ALUF) can be obtained to process F store contents directly with 16 possible functions. The function is specified indirectly (AUX3) and the output is obtained by an IN0 transfer from ALUF (indicated in AUX0) to another F.

7.2.7 Nano Store

The last major functional unit of the QM-1 to be described is the nano store (NS). A full word in nano store is 360 bits, made up of a 72-bit K vector and four 72-bit T vectors as will be described in the following section (7.3). Nano store is available in 256 word blocks, up to a limit of 1,024 words. Blocks are further subdivided into 128 word pages.

Nanoprimitives READ NS, WRITE NS, and GATE NS are available, providing the nanoprogrammer with the capability to dynamically alter the contents of nano store as well as to read out selected locations on command. A WRITE NS operation can only alter 18 bits of a 360-bit word. For this purpose, a nanoword can be considered to be composed of 20 units of 18 bits each (0–19). The 10-bit address is taken from R31 (bits 15-6, from C and A fields), the 18-bit-unit number from the B field (low order 5 bits), and the actual data to be written from the EOD bus.

The detailed breakout of nanoword contents is described in the following section, along with an examination of the nanocontrol structure.

7.3 NANOINSTRUCTIONS AND NANO LEVEL CONTROL

It has already been pointed out that the nano level control is horizontal and closely associated with low level hardware operations. Many of the individual nano level commands have been described along with the hardware features to which they pertain. This section

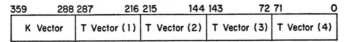

Fig. 7-4: Format of the 360-Bit Nanoword.

will examine the nanoinstruction as an entity and further describe the overall nano level control structure with emphasis on the sequential occurrence of control actions.

7.3.1 Nanoinstruction Formats

The concept of a nanoinstruction in the QM-1 is somewhat unusual, in that a nanoinstruction does not correspond directly to a nanoword. In fact, the term *nanoinstruction* is not generally used by the manufacturer; essentially, it can be equated to the combination of the K vector with the *active* T vector as will become clear. (The nanoword may alternatively be considered to be a variation on the "polyphase" nanoinstruction.)

A 360-bit nanoword contains the 72-bit K vector and four 72-bit T vectors as shown in Figure 7-4. At any one time, machine operations are controlled by the K vector and one of the T vectors. K vector field assignments are detailed in Table 7-2, while Figure 7-2 provides additional details of fields within the K vector. Nanoprimitive fields of the T vector are similarly detailed in Table 7-3.

The high incidence of single-bit fields in the K and T vectors is indicative of the hardware level of control. Longer bit fields employ some encoding to reduce field width; nevertheless, little flexibility is sacrificed since many encoded options are inherently mutually exclusive.

7.3.2 Timing

The QM-1 CPU operates in a synchronous mode with a basic machine clock period of 80 nanoseconds. A "T period" is equal to the length of a machine clock period. Normally a single T vector remains active for a single T period, but, by use of the STRETCH field in the T vector, it may be extended to two T periods as is required for certain operations.

Another factor that must be considered by the nanoprogrammer is the subcycle time at which any nanoprimitive takes effect. Thus~ nanoprimitives are generally classified as leading edge (LE) or trailing edge (TE), according to whether they take effect at the beginning of a T period or at the end; this information is included in Table 7-3.

7.3.3 Nanoinstruction Sequencing and Control

Sequencing

In lieu of a nanoinstruction register, the QM-1 has a *control matrix* which holds a full nanoword with a K vector and four T vectors (Figure 7-4). When the nanoword is loaded into the control matrix, its K vector becomes active along with the first T vector (T1). With no further intervention, successive T vectors become active with each new T period (unless STRETCHed), while the K vector remains active. This continues in cyclic rotation (T1, T2, T3, T4, T1, T2, and so on) until a new nanoword is loaded and the process starts over with a new K vector and a new T1 vector. Note that it is thus possible to have useful program loops within a single nanoword.

The normal cyclic process can be broken in one of two ways: A Program Check interrupt can occur, or the nanoprogram can cause a new nanoword to be loaded. Interrupts will be discussed next in section 7.3.4.

When a new word has been read from nanostore, it is not automatically loaded into the control matrix. A new word is not loaded until the GATE NS nanoprimitive is executed; since GATE NS is a trailing edge action, the new nanoword will take effect at the beginning of the following T period.

The GATE NS UNCONDITIONALLY nanoprimitive may be used to load a new nanoword, or for conditional loading, the GATE NS option in the TEST ACTION field is available. The TEST ACTION function will conditionally occur according to the results of the test specified by TEST SPECIFIER. Testable fields include global conditions in FIST (Figure 7-3 and section 7.2.1), local conditions, and special conditions (Figure 7-5). The K vector may contain masks to be applied for selecting specific test conditions: KS masks global conditions, KT masks local conditions, and KX masks special conditions.

As an alternative to the conditional loading of the control matrix, the TEST ACTION option of SKIP may be used to conditionally

Table 7-2: Fields of Nanoinstruction K Vector (Courtesy Nanodata Corp.).

CONTROL FIELD	BITS	SUMMARY OF CONTROL FUNCTION
KN	(10)	Address of possible successor nanoword. Nanobranch address and source for MPC load.
SUPERVISOR	(1)	Program Check if on when this word is invoked while not in Supervisor Mode.
LEGAL MICRO ENTRY	(1)	Program Check if not on when this word is invoked by a microinstruction.
BRANCH	(1)	Must be on if nanobranch planned from this word. Complemented after each READ NS when ALTERNATE is on.
ALTERNATE	(1)	Causes BRANCH to be complemented after each READ NS.
HOLD	(1)	Inhibits automatic loading of KALC, KSHC, KSHA, and KS from next nanoword to be executed, unless executed by microinstruction or Program Check.
HOLD 2	(1)	Inhibits automatic loading of KA and KB from next nanoword to be executed, unless executed by microinstruction or Program Check.
ALLOW NANO INTERRUPT	(1)	Allows higher priority interrupts at end of execution of this word, if nanobranch is not taken.
ALLOW MICRO INTERRUPT	(1)	Allows lower priority interrupts at end of execution of this word, if nanobranch is not taken.
GENERATE INTERRUPT	(1)	Generates or clears an interrupt level according to G1(GSPEC1) in T1.
ALU STATUS ENABLE	(1)	Enables move of C,S,R,O bits from local to global upon GATE ALU; C treated specially.
SH STATUS ENABLE	(1)	Enables move of SHB, SLB bits from local to global upon GATE SH.
DIRECT MX ACCESS	(1)	Inhibits MS base addressing and field length protection in this nanoword.

(Continued)

Table 7-2 (Continued)

CONTROL FIELD	BITS	SUMMARY OF CONTROL FUNCTION
KA	(6)	Constant and/or scratch field for nanoword; source and destination AUX.
KB	(6)	Constant and/or scratch field for nanoword; source and destination AUX.
KALC	(6)	ALU control; destination AUX.
KSHC	(6)	Shift control; destination AUX.
KSHA	(6)	Shift amount; destination AUX.
KS	(6)	Global condition (and general) test mask; source and destination AUX.
KT	(6)	Local condition test mask (also constant and/or scratch); source and destination AUX.
KX	(6)	Special condition test mask (also constant and/or scratch); source and destination AUX.
SPARE	(2)	Reserved for future use.
K Vector Total 72 Bits		

skip the next T vector. The same tests apply as for GATE NS. Note that by using GATE NS UNCONDITIONALLY and SKIP, it is possible to conditionally skip the T1 vector of the new nanoword.

Nanoword Address Selection

The QM-1 effectively maintains a priority ordered list of possible sources for the address of the next nanoword. These include, in order of descending priority: program check (internal interrupts), nanobranch, external interrupts, and the nanoprogram counter (NPC). When a READ NS is executed, possible address sources are scanned in priority sequence and the highest priority source that has been enabled supplies the address for the read. Program checks and interrupts will be described in the following section.

If the BRANCH bit in the K vector is on and no program checks exist, the read address will be taken from the KN field in the K vector; the ALTERNATE field provides for clearing this bit after alternate READ NS operations (assuming no GATE NS).

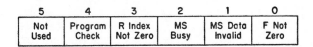

5	4	3	2	1	0
Not Used	Program Check	R Index Not Zero	MS Busy	MS Data Invalid	F Not Zero

Fig. 7-5: Special Conditions Masking Format.

Lowest priority address source is the nanoprogram counter. This counter is maintained under nanoprogram control by use of the LOAD NPC nanoprimitive. The NPC can be loaded from any of three sources. CS option creates an address from the nano store page index in FIDX (Figure 7-3) (3 bits) and the 7-bit microopcode (assumed to be on the COD bus); this provides entry to a nanoprogram for microinstruction interpretation. KN option loads the NPC from the KN field of the K vector and is functionally equivalent to BRANCH. Finally, SEQUENCE increments the current NPC value by 1 for sequencing through successive nano store locations.

Micro Level Architecture Support

Loading the NPC with the CS option has been described as the principal method of branching to nanoprogram routines for micro-instruction interpretation. It should be noted that neither this branching method nor the availability of R31 as the MIR unduly constrain the range of micro level architectures that can be supported. Microinstructions can be of arbitrary length with arbitrary field assignments; it may be necessary, however, to do some manipulation of the actual fields in order to take full advantage of the QM-1 hardware.

The complete set of nanoprimitives available combined with the maskable condition fields provide an extremely flexible set of alternatives for nanoinstruction sequencing. Any desired macro level or micro level sequencing scheme can readily be supported. Also, alternative branching methods (with and without NPC) readily facilitate subroutine structures within nanoprograms.

7.3.4 Program Checks and Interrupts

Program checks are *hard* interrupts caused by internal QM-1 conditions: MS parity error; MS address error; illegal microoperation entry; privileged operation (supervisory) error; and nanoprogram (microinstruction) time out. The latter prevents hanging up in tight loops. These conditions result in automatic transfers to a program

Table 7-3: Fields of Nanoinstruction T Vector (Nanoprimitives) (Courtesy Nanodata Corp.).

CONTROL FIELD	BITS	SUMMARY OF CONTROL FUNCTION	TIME
STRETCH	(1)	Stretches time of this T step from one T period to two.	
WRITE NS	(1)	Writes 18 bits from EOD bus into Nanostore.	LE
XIO	(1)	Sends pulse to external interface; one of eight external ports selected by KA.	LE
RIO	(1)	Clears Port Register and sends pulse through port, then gates external data word into Port Register; selected by KA.	LE
MSGO	(1)	Initiates MS operation; split-cycle if alone, full-read if MSRS simultaneous.	LE
MSRS	(1)	If alone, requests second half-cycle of MS split-cycle operation; if with MSGO, initiates full-read.	LE
GATE MS	(1)	Gates MOD bus into Local Store or Port Registers; modified by RMI SELECT.	TE
RMI SELECT 00 BYPASS 01 PARAMETER SET A 10 PARAMETER SET B 11 PARAMETER SET C	(2)	Selects RMI parameters for GATE MS, including BYPASS. If RMI not installed all encodings are BYPASS	LE
GATE ES	(1)	Gates EOD bus into Local Store.	TE
LOAD ES	(1)	Loads an External Store register from EID bus.	TE
TXX	(1)	Halts T-Clock with Program Step Switch.	TE
READ CS	(1)	Reads Control Store; uses CS ADDR SELECT.	LE
WRITE CS	(1)	Writes Control Store; uses CSADDN Select.	LE

(Continued)

CONTROL FIELD	BITS	SUMMARY OF CONTROL FUNCTION	TIME
CS ADDR SELECT 000 CIA 001 COD 010 MPC 011 MPC+1 100 MPC+2 101 MPC+B 110 MPC+AB 111 INDEX	(3)	Selects address for READ CS, WRITE CS. (MPC is selected by FMPC.) A and AB are sign extended operands. INDEX is output of INDEX ALU.	LE
GATE CS	(1)	Gates COD bus into Local Store.	TE
GATE ALU	(1)	Gates AOD bus into Local Store.	TE
GATE SH	(1)	Gates SOD bus into Local Store.	TE
CARRY CTL 000 NO OPERATION 001 CLEAR CIH 010 SET CIH 011 ALU TO BOTH 100 ALU TO COH 101 SET COH 110 CLEAR COH 111 SH TO COH	(3)	Controls Carry operation within the ALU and Shifter components.	TE
INDEX	(1)	Gates INDEX ALU output into Local Store, selected by G(GSPEC).	TE
INC MPC	(1)	Increments MPC selected by FMPC; modified by GSPEC.	TE
LOAD NPC 00 NO OPERATION 01 (CS) 10 (KN) 11 (Sequence)	(2)	Loads or sequences Nano Program Counter.	TE
READ NS	(1)	Reads NS; address is from priority-select mechanism. Influences BRANCH.	LE
GATE NS UNCON- DITIONALLY	(1)	Causes the nanoword last read to be gated into the Control Matrix. Independent of any TEST ACTION in T.	TE

(Continued)

Table 7-3 (Continued)

CONTROL FIELD	BITS	SUMMARY OF CONTROL FUNCTION	TIME
TEST ACTION 0 SKIP 1 GATE NS	(1)	Conditional Action based on Test Specifier.	TE
TEST SPECIFIER 000 NEVER 001 ALWAYS 010 If FIST AND KS = 0 011 If FIST AND KS NOT = 0 100 If LOCAL CONDS AND KT = 0 101 If LOCAL CONDS AND KT NOT = 0 110 If SPECIAL CONDS AND KX = 0 111 If SPECIAL CONDS AND KX NOT = 0	(3)	Specifies the conditions under which TEST ACTION is to be executed.	LE
LOAD R31	(1)	Enables R31 to be loaded with micro- instruction parameters.	TE
AUXILLARY ACTION	(1)	Initiates Action specified by the contents of FACT (F register 14).	LE
GSPEC 0000 G0 ⋮ ⋮ 1011 G11 1100 KSHA 1101 B 1110 KS 1111 KT	(4)	Selects a G or pseudo-G for 6 bit transfers, right input to ALUF, used in GENERATE INTERRUPT, External interface G-lines; also used with INC MPC.	
FSEL0 FSEL1 FSEL2	(5) (5) (5)	Selects F register for 6 bit transfers in Group 0, 1, and 2 respectively.	
AUX0 AUX1 AUX2 AUX3	(3) (3) (3) (3)	Selects AUX for 6 bit transfers in Group 0, 1, and 2 respectively. (AUX2 applies to Group 2 input, AUX3 applies to Group 2 output.)	
IN0 IN1 IN2	(1) (1) (1)	Commands AUX into F register transfer using AUX0, AUX1, AUX2 to FSEL0, FSEL1, FSEL2, respectively.	
OUT1 OUT2 OUT3	(1) (1) (1)	Commands F register output to AUX transfer using FSEL0, FSEL1, FSEL2 to AUX0, AUX1, AUX3 respectively.	
T Vector Total 72 Bits			

check service nanoprogram that resides in a special 32-word read-only nano store (RONS) separate from the regular NS. Contents of RONS is customer specified, and access is controlled by the NS mode bit of FIDX (Figure 7-3).

External interrupts are only partially *soft* in that the nanoprogrammer has limited control over their handling. Hardware automatically causes a transfer of control when an external interrupt is pending (assuming, of course, that no higher priority NS address source is active and the external interrupt has also been enabled). Subsequent actions are at the discretion of the nanoprogrammer.

A total of 30 levels of external interrupts are provided in priority order. The highest ten levels are considered as nano interrupts and the lower 20 as micro interrupts; enabling of these two groups is separately controllable through the nanoprimitives, ALLOW NANO INTERRUPT and ALLOW MICRO INTERRUPT at the group level, and through individual bits in external store registers E18 and E19 at the individual interrupt level. Auxiliary action (FACT, section 7.2.7) commands are also available to disable/enable all I/O interrupts with a single command.

It was mentioned earlier in section 7.2.3 that external store registers E22–E31 contain compacted addresses to be used for handling interrupts. Each 18-bit word contains three 6-bit compacted addresses that are expanded into ten NS addresses by the insertion of zeros (viz. abcdef → 0ab000cdef), such that each page of NS has 16 possible interrupt entry addresses. Level assignments are made during installation, while address assignments and handling routines are the responsibility of the nanoprogrammer.

The K vector includes a GENERATE INTERRUPT field that permits the nanoprogrammer to artificially generate an external interrupt and/or clear one. The GSPEC field is used to select the desired level and to specify the generate or clear action.

7.4 INPUT/OUTPUT

The QM-1 I/O system is shown in block diagram form in Figure 7-6. The CPU has eight I/O ports (as described in section 7.2.3), with an 18-bit external store interface register for each. Used in conjunction with the external interrupt system, the port registers permit control over multiple simultaneous I/O operations.

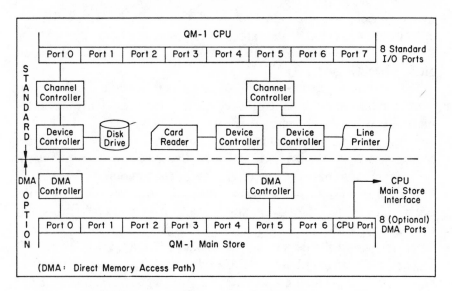

Fig. 7-6: QM-1 I/O System (Courtesy Nanodata Corp.).

One channel controller may connect to each port, with up to.64 device controllers on a channel. Since some device controllers can control multiple devices, it is possible to have more than 64 devices on a single channel.

Main store may be obtained with up to eight ports also (QM-1 option). With one port reserved for normal access by the CPU, up to seven memory ports are thus available for connection to direct memory access (DMA) controllers. This capability combined with the standard I/O ports allows a wide range of I/O options.

7.5 ORGANIZATIONAL PARAMETERS

The basic internal clock period of 80 nanoseconds has already been mentioned. Nanoprimitives execute in either 80 or 160 nanoseconds (T period or STRETCHed T period).

Main store has access and cycle times of 640 ns. and 800 ns. respectively. Cycle times for control store and nano store are 75 nanoseconds.

7.6 SUMMARY

The QM-1 architecture is ideally suited to a research environment because of the multiple levels of control provided. Experiments on design of micro level architectures can readily be conducted, with the advantage of having the macro level available also for benchmark application/target machine programs for execution/emulation.

The difficulties of nanoprogramming the QM-1 are at least partially offset by the availability of a nano assembler, with special capabilities to assist specifically in defining a micro level architecture. In addition, a standard micro level emulator (implemented via nanoprogram) called "MULTI" is provided to preclude the necessity of writing nanoprograms. MULTI is a vertically structured system which takes advantage of many of the nano level features and is particularly well suited for emulation applications. Of course, the possible uses of the machine are not restricted to macro or micro level emulation by any means. Taking full advantage of all of the resources provided by this machine is, nevertheless, a challenging task.

As this is written, several machines have been installed and others are on order, within military research facilities, universities and industry. Whether or not such an architecture can profitably be utilized in a commercial production environment remains to be seen.

Chapter 8
Other Architectures

8.1 INTRODUCTION

The architectures presented in depth in the preceeding chapters represent significantly different architectural approaches in the design of microprogrammable computers. They are neither exhaustive of the approaches that can and have been taken, nor do they necessarily represent the mainstream of current or future machine popularity.

To add greater depth and balance to the overall range of architectures considered in this book, this chapter includes brief overviews of an additional six machines. The first four—CDC 5600, Digital Scientific META 4, Hewlett Packard 2100/21MX, and Varian 73—have been selected primarily on the basis of their past, current, or anticipated popularity for general purpose microprogramming and emulation. The last two—INTEL 3000 and Western Digital MCP 1600— are included as representatives of the new wave, microprogrammable microprocessors! Available as LSI chip sets, these new microprocessors can be expected to serve as the basis for new macro level machines, for emulators of existing machines, and as flexible building blocks for a range of microprogrammed devices.

Collectively these architectures, when added to the four previously presented, should round out the reader's perspective in the architecture of microprogrammable computers. Sufficient similarities and differences can be identified within the total set to serve as a basis for further analysis and comparisons.

8.2 CONTROL DATA 5600

The Control Data 5600 is another machine with no specified macro level instruction set. It is a general purpose microprogrammable processor (MPP) with several features making it particularly well suited to emulation applications.

The architecture of the 5600 (Figure 8-1) provides for a modularly expandable data width of from 8 to 32 bits in 4 bit increments. Microinstructions are basically vertical, with parallelism limited to simultaneous I/O or memory actions along with ALU operations and next microinstruction selection. Each microinstruction (Figure 8-2) is 32 bits in length, selecting A and B inputs to the ALU from among the six principal registers and register files, as well as specifying an ALU function and output destination.

The ALU operates in 1's or 2's complement mode as specified by the microprogrammer. Options available include double precision hardware and a "split" mode allowing simultaneous ALU operation on independent upper and lower halves of the inputs.

The six basic registers are all general purpose, but their names indicate typical usage during emulation; I normally holds the current macro level instruction and P holds the macro level program address; A and Q can be combined to form a double word AQ, and either A or AQ can be shifted (without the ALU) by the count in the N register; X is general purpose with no special use; and F holds information to be stored in the file registers. Two register files are available; file 1 consists of 256 word-length registers and file 2 has 32 word-length registers normally used for frequently needed constants.

The N and K registers are each 8-bit control registers. K selects file 1 registers and also serves as a general utility counter. N selects file 2 registers, acts as a "repeat" control to cause repeated execution of a microinstruction pair, and as a counter controls A and AQ shift functions. Other registers include status/mode (SM) for 1's, 2's complement mode selection, interrupt enable, ALU status, and so on; MASK for individual interrupt enabling; P and MA for selection of the current microinstruction pair with a counter (MAC) for incremental sequencing; a *bit generator* to generate full words with a single 1 bit present; and a return jump (RTJ) register for microprogram address storage such as used in subroutine control.

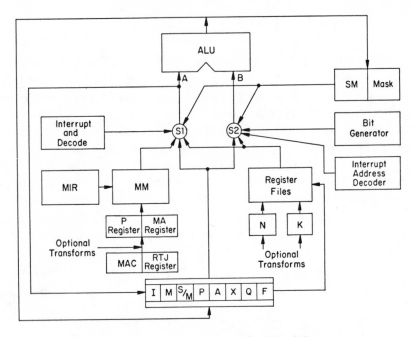

Fig. 8-1: Control Data 5600 Simplified Block Diagram
(Courtesy Control Data Corp.).

An important option available for dedicated emulation usage is the *transform* module that can be custom designed to extract given bits from selected registers, shift as required, add base addresses or constants, and transfer resulting data to MAC, K, and N registers. These functions can significantly improve emulation efficiency by performing many of the target instruction decode operations.

Control store can be either ROM or read-write. Available sizes range from 256 to 4K words, each containing two 32-bit microinstructions with a cycle time of 80 nanoseconds.

8.3 DIGITAL SCIENTIFIC META 4

The META 4 (Figure 8-3) is a 16-bit processor from the Digital Scientific Corporation designed for general purpose microprogramming rather than implementation of a particular macro level architecture. It has been actively marketed by Digital Scientific as an emulator for the IBM 1130 and 1800 systems.

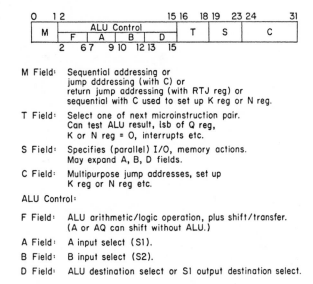

Fig. 8-2: Control Data 5600 Microinstruction Format.

Microinstructions (Figure 8-4) for the META 4 are 32 bits wide, highly encoded with four formats, and are essentially vertical in structure. Separate fields specify the basic operation to be performed, registers to be used as A and B sources and destination, I/O and memory control, and special controls for microinstruction looping and arithmetic/shift options.

The arithmetic/boolean unit ALU performs 16 basic functions with detailed carry options controllable by the microprogrammer. The skew (shifter) unit can shift either 1 or 8 bits left or right. Sign Extend and Scale (one place end-off right shift with arithmetic carry into left) shift commands are also available.

The basic META 4 has four registers: all zeros in register 0, Condition/Counter register 1, Link register 2, and a general purpose register 3. This set can be expanded to 32 with various combinations of additional general purpose registers, I/O register pairs, and memory register pairs, as well as indirectly addressable scratchpad registers.

Control store for the META 4 is novel and fast (90 nanosecond access). Individual bits are alterable through positioning of removable adhesive-bonded metallic "bit patch" patterns that can be done by users in the field. Capacity is from 1 to 4K words of 16 bits each (two per microinstruction) in 1K increments.

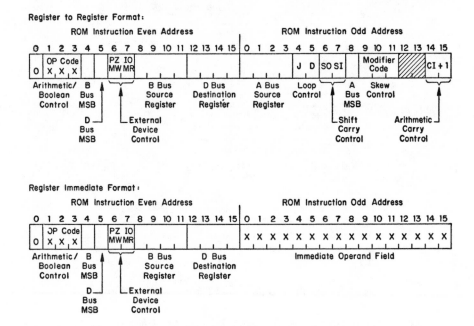

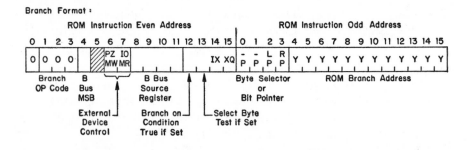

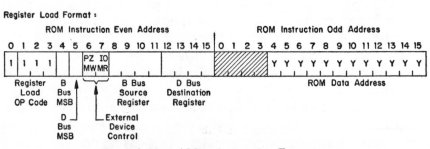

Fig. 8-4: Meta 4 Microinstruction Formats
(Courtesy Digital Scientific Corp.).

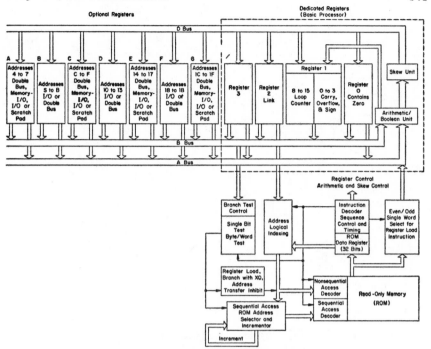

Fig. 8-3: Meta 4 System Block Diagram
(Courtesy Digital Scientific Corp.).

8.4 HEWLETT PACKARD 2100 AND 21MX

The HP2100 (Figure 8-5) and HP21MX (Figure 8-6) are both microprogrammable processors that implement a common compatible basic set of macro (machine) level instructions, employing somewhat different architectures. The newer of the two is the 21MX, with a larger complement of registers, increased control store size, and simplified bus structure as compared to the 2100. The basic instruction set is fixed and standard, with writable control store available to provide extensions or otherwise allow user microprogramming.

Both machines utilize 24-bit vertical type microinstructions, with a fixed format in the 2100 and four formats (more encoding) for the 21MX. The formats are illustrated in Figure 8-7. In the 2100, the R bus and S bus fields gate specified registers onto their associated buses, and the store field gates the ALU/shifter output from the T bus back into a selected register, while the Function field controls the

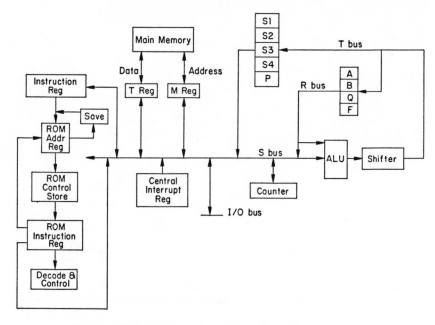

Fig. 8-5: HP2100 Micro Level Block Diagram.

ALU and shifter operation. The 21MX uses the S bus and Store fields in a similar manner, but the second ALU input is from the L register in lieu of an R bus. In both machines the Store field can also be used to store the contents of the S bus in one of its connected registers. While the lack of an R bus in the 21 MX appears to cause a loss in flexibility and power compared to the 2100, the additional power of the more complex microinstruction format set and the improved hardware performance of the 21MX more than compensate for this lack. In general, the 21MX will out perform the 2100 on complex instructions, while it may take longer than the 2100 on simple instructions.

Functional units for data transformation in both machines consist of the ALU and shifter. The 2100 microinstruction has only the 5-bit Function field (plus the Special field) to control operations, while the 21MX, by virtue of its greater degree of encoding in microinstructions, enjoys a 5-bit ALU field as well as a 4-bit Operation field permitting more complex operations to be controlled.

The A and B registers in both machines are for use as target

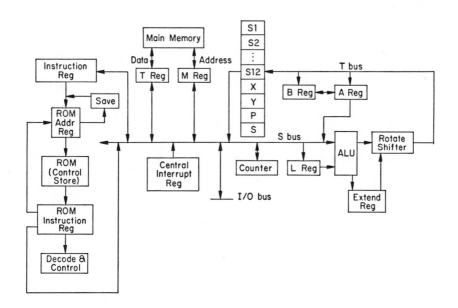

Fig. 8-6: HP21MX Micro Level Block Diagram

(macro) level registers; the P register serves as the macro level program counter and the instruction register holds target level instructions. The 21MX has 12 scratchpad registers compared to the 2100's four, and, unlike the 2100, the 21MX scratchpad registers can be read from and written into during a single microcycle. The Q and F registers of the 2100 and the X and Y registers of the 21MX provide extra general registers for use by the microprogrammer which in both machines can be used to read from and write back into during the same microinstruction.

Control store for the 2100 consists of four modules of 256 words each, with module 0 dedicated to implementation of the basic instruction set; the remaining three modules are available for options, extensions, and user microprograms. A console switch permits substitution of a different module zero as well. The 21MX can have up to 16 control store modules, with four (0, 1, 14, 15) reserved for the basic instruction set plus extensions. Significantly greater user microprogramming facilities are thus available with the HP21MX machine.

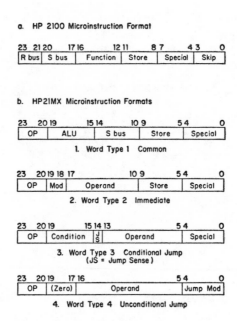

a. HP 2100 Microinstruction Format

b. HP21MX Microinstruction Formats

1. Word Type 1   Common

2. Word Type 2   Immediate

3. Word Type 3   Conditional Jump
(JS = Jump Sense)

4. Word Type 4   Unconditional Jump

Fig. 8-7: HP2100 and HP21MX Microinstruction

8.5 VARIAN 73

The Varian 73 (Figure 8-8) is a general purpose microprogrammable processor with a 16-bit data width. Although the typical processor includes a read-only-memory (firmware) control store to emulate the Varian 620 series machines, the inclusion of writable control store facilities and the flexibility of the basic architecture combine to permit the extension of the 620 repertoire, the emulation of other target machines, and general applications microprogramming as well.

The wide 64-bit microinstruction includes 25 individual fields with the potential for simultaneous control of several different functions, making the machine fall into the horizontal classification. The fields are not all independent, however; not only is encoding used within many of the fields, but in addition the meaning of a field is frequently conditioned by the contents of another field.

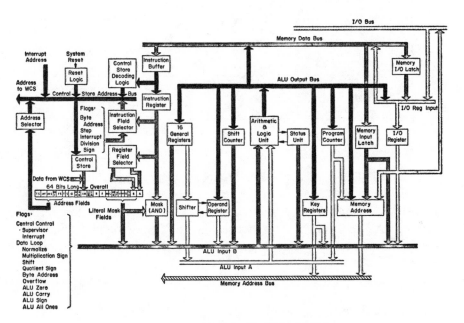

Fig. 8-8: Varian 73 Processor Block Diagram
(Courtesy of Varian Data Machines).

Basic fundamental facilities include a multifunction ALU with status unit and controllable carry input, and a single bit shifter that functions on the A input to the ALU or with the operand register. A separate shift counter facilitates ALU/shift control. The general register file includes 16 general registers. Target instruction emulation is aided by the program counter, instruction register, and operand register. In addition, the ability to selectively extract and mask fields from the instruction register further assists the emulation process.

Writable control store options include a separate writable decoder control store (another bonus for general emultation) and a writable I/O control store for additional flexibility. A subroutine stack to hold return microprogram addresses is a standard feature. Each

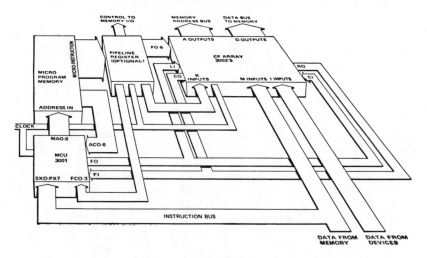

Fig. 8-9: Typical Intel 3000 Microcomputer Configuration.

microinstruction contains several fields and test conditions used in determining the control store address of the following microinstruction. The instruction buffer permits an overlap of target instruction fetching and executing.

8.6 INTEL 3000

The Intel 3000 series is a set of LSI components for assembling microprogrammed processors and microcomputers. The two principal members of the family are the 3001 Microprogram Control Unit (MCU) and the 3002 Central Processing Element (CPE). Each CPE is a 2-bit slice, many of which can be arrayed together to construct a processor of arbitrary word length (theoretically up to 320 bits). A variety of ROM's and PROM's (programmable ROM's) are available for control memory purposes, as well as additional ancillary packages to permit design of more powerful or faster microcomputers (for example, look-ahead carry generators, priority interrupt control units, and so on).

A typical 3000 system is illustrated in Figure 8-9. It consists of a single MCU, an array of n CPE's (n = wordlength/2), a control memory, and a *pipeline* register that allows overlap of current microinstruction execution and next microinstruction fetch.

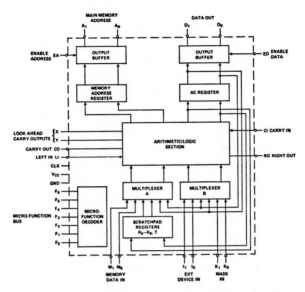

Fig. 8-10a: 3002 Central Processing Element (CPE).

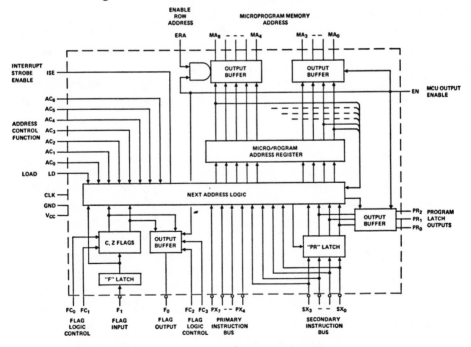

Fig. 8-10b: 3001 Microprogram Control Unit (MCU).
Fig. 8-10: Intel 3000 Series Block Diagrams
(Courtesy Intel Corp.).

The 2-bit slice CPE (Figure 8-10a) consists of an arithmetic/logic section (ALS) capable of performing over 40 boolean and binary functions, two multiplexers for selecting A and B ALS inputs, an accumulator (AC) register and memory address register for ALS outputs, and an 11-register scratchpad file. Three input buses permit ALS input selection from memory data in, external device in, and the K bus (mask), in addition to the scratchpad registers (R0–R9 plus T), AC and ALS output. The mask input on the K bus originates from a mask field in the microinstruction; the B multiplexer outputs are always ANDed with this mask, adding great versatility to the functions the microprogrammer can perform using the CPE. Another novel CPE feature is the provision for *conditional clocking,* which in effect freezes the clock, allowing an operation to be performed and carry or shift data to be generated for test, while at the same time prohibiting the results from being actually clocked into the specified registers and potentially saving both microinstructions and execution time.

The function of the MCU (Figure 8-10b) is to develop microinstruction addresses based on the previous microinstruction, flags (from carry/shift operations), and selected bits from the secondary (that is, macro level) instruction from main memory. Control memory addresses are based on a row/column matrix addressing scheme with a basic 512 location control memory organized into 32 rows and 16 columns; the *jump set* of possible next microinstruction instruction addresses is limited to being within the current row or current column for unconditional jumps, while conditional jump sets are less restrictive. Additional planes of 512 locations may be added.

Microinstruction length (Figure 8-11) will be determined by the system configuration and desires of the designer. The minimum microinstruction is 18 bits in length and is vertical in structure. Three bits of the CPE function field select the ALS function group, and 4 bits select the register group; the actual complete function performed is dependent upon the function group, the register group, and the K bus contents. The remaining 11 bits control the flag options and jump function. The mask field will be the same width as the data width of the CPE array; optional processor function bits include functions such as conditional clocking.

Properly configured, the 3000 series can cover a broad range of microprogramming applications, including general purpose emula-

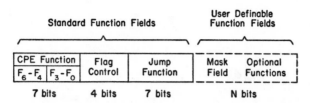

Fig. 8-11: Intel 3000 Microinstruction Format.

tion. The technology employed makes 125 nanosecond microinstruction execution times readily achievable, according to the manufacturer.

8.7 WESTERN DIGITAL MCP 1600

The MCP 1600 from Western Digital is a 3 chip microprocessor set that is microprogrammable. Designed as a microprogrammable processor for direct applications microprogramming or for emulation of an arbitrary macro level instruction set, it has already been used for a microprocessor emulation of the DEC PDP-11 instruction set.

The architecture of the chip set (Figure 8-12) is divided into a data chip, a control chip, and one or more MICROM control store chips. Interchip communication is via the 18-bit microinstruction bus (MIB). The vertical microinstructions are encoded in four formats (Figure 8-13), with the basic microinstruction occupying 16 bits, 2 additional bits for special control functions, and 4 additional user bits to be defined by the microprogrammer (not available on the bus).

While the ALU is byte oriented, microinstructions may call for either byte or word (16-bit) operations, the latter simply requiring two cycles to complete. An added feature is the availability for test of the carry out from the fourth bit (bit 3) and eighth bit from the ALU to facilitate decimal arithmetic. Inputs to the ALU include two ports from the register file (a and b) and the output is fed back to the register file (a). In addition to 4 micro level ALU status bits, the data chip includes 4 macro level status bits controllable by the microprogram for emulation usage.

The register file includes a total of 26 8-bit registers, some of which can be paired for 16-bit operands. Fourteen registers are

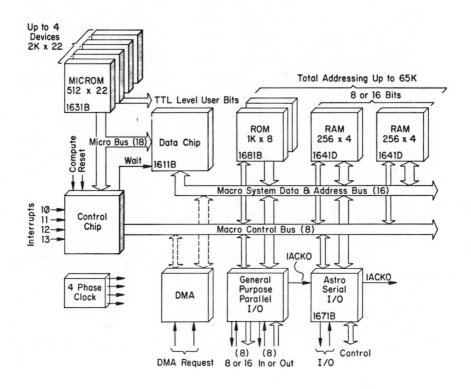

Fig. 8-12a: MCP1600 Block Diagram
(Courtesy Western Digital Corp.).

directly addressable, while eight pairs may be indirectly addressed using the G register. The G register (3 bits) may be explicitly loaded under microprogram control or, alternatively, may be implicitly loaded with user designated bits from the macro level instruction when that instruction is read.

The control chip includes the translation register (TR)—along with the translation state register (TSR) to develop jump addresses directly from macro level instructions for instruction decoding. The TR holds the macro level instruction word and presents it to the programmable translation array (PTA), a user specifiable array unit. The location counter (LC) holds the address of the next micro-

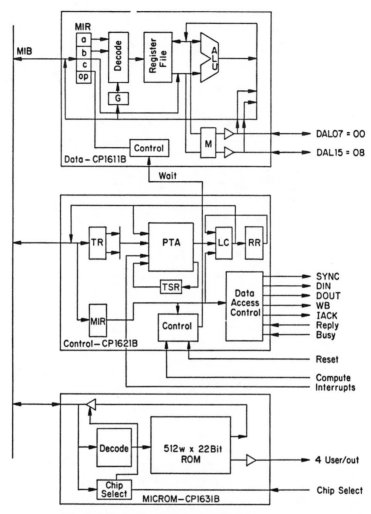

Fig. 8-12b: MCP 1600 System Diagram
(Courtesy Western Digital Corp.).

instruction to be executed, and the return register (RR) is used to store the return address from micro level subroutines.

Each MICROM chip holds 512 microinstructions of 22 bits each. Up to four chips may be included. Support available from Western Digital (via time sharing) includes a microprogram assembler for both the MICROM and PTA, as well as a full simulator to check out microprograms prior to committing to production.

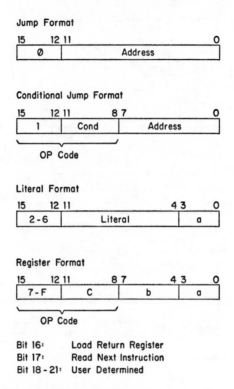

Fig. 8-13: MCP 1600 Microinstruction Formats.

8.8 SUMMARY

In many respects microprogramming has matured in recent years. No longer the exclusive province of the computer designer, it is now a tool available to systems designers, systems programmers, and applications programmers alike.

The range of microprogrammable computer architectures currently available is very broad and can be expected to expand further. The architectures presented in this book provide a good representative cross section of the state of the art. As new architectures arrive on the scene, they can be better understood and appreciated by comparing them to those included here.

Bibliography

This bibliography includes detailed reference citations for all works cited within the text, as well as many other important papers and books pertaining to microprogramming in general and micro level architecture in particular.

For those wishing to pursue any topic related to microprogramming in more depth, the reference listed as SIGM74 should be of particular interest. This reference is to a special "Bibliography on Microprogramming" issue of the *SIGMICRO Newsletter,* including a key word in context (KWIC) listing. Inquiries as to availability of SIGMICRO publications should be directed to:

> The Association for Computing Machinery
> 1133 Avenue of the Americas
> New York, N.Y. 10036.

AGRA74   Agrawala, A. K., and Rauscher, T. G. "Microprogramming: Perspective and Status," *IEEE Transactions on Computers,* August 1974: 817–837.

AMDA64   Amdahl, Lowell D. "Microprogramming and Stored Logic." *Datamation* 10, no. 2 (February 1964): 24–26.

BARS71   Barsamian, H. and DeCegana, A. "Evaluation of Hardware-Firmware-Software Tradeoffs with Mathematical Modelling." *Proceedings of the AFIPS Conference* 38(SJCC) (1971): 151–161.

BAZE60   Bazerque, G.; Ferrie, J; and Hugot, P. "Universal Micromachine Structure Study Oriented to Simulation of Computers." *Information Processing* 68 (Amsterdam: North-Holland Publishing Company, 1969).

BEEL67   Beelitz, H. R.; Levy, S. Y.; Linhardt, R. J.; and Miller, H. S. "System Architecture for Large Scale Integration." *Proceedings of the AFIPS Conference* 31(FJCC) (1967): 185–200.

BELL71   Bell, C. G., and Newell, A. *Computer Structures: Readings and Examples.* New York: McGraw-Hill, 1971.

BURN73   Burns, R., and Savitt, D. "Microprogramming, Stack Architecture Ease Minicomputer Programmers Burden." *Electronics,* February 15, 1973: 95–101.

BURR72   Burroughs Corporation. *Burroughs B1700 Systems Reference Manual,* preliminary ed., 1972.

CASA71   Casaglia, G. F.; Gerace, G. B.; and Vanneschi, M. *Equivalent Models and Comparison of Microprogrammed Systems.* Grenoble: NATO International Advanced Summer Institute on Microprogramming, August 30–September 10, 1971.

CASH71   Cashman, M. W. "Microprogramming for the Many." *Datamation,* November 1, 1972: 32.

CDCM72   Control Data Corporation. *Reference Manual, CDC 5600 Series of Microprogrammable Processors,* no. 14232000 (1972).

CLAP72   Clapp, J. A. "The Application of Microprogramming Technology." *SIGMICRO Newsletter* 3, no. 1 (April 1972): 8–47.

CLAR72   Clark, R. K. "Mirager, the 'Best-Yet' Approach for Horizontal Microprogramming." *Proceedings of the ACM Annual Conference,* August 1972: 541–571.

COOK70   Cook, R. W., and Flynn, M. J. "System Design of a Dynamic Microprocessor." *IEEE Transactions on Computers* C-19, no. 3 (March 1970): 213–222.

DAVI71   Davis, R. L., and Zucker, S. "Structure of a Multi-Processor Using Microprogrammable Building Blocks." *SIGMICRO Newsletter* 2, no. 3 (October 1971): 27–42.

DAVP72   Davies, P. M. "Readings in Microprogramming." *IBM Systems Journal,* no. 1 (1972): 16–40.

DIGI72A   Digital Scientific Corporation. *META 4 Computer System Microprogramming Reference Manual,* June 1972.

DSCM72   Digital Scientific Corporation. *Microprogramming Reference Manual, META 4 Computer System,* no. 7043MO (1972).

DREY68   Dreyer, L. "Principles of a Two-Level Memory Computer." *Computers and Automation* 17, no. 5 (May 1968): 40–42.

EMEL62   Emelyanov-Yaroslavsky, L. B., and Timofeev, A. A. "Microprogram Control for Digital Computers." *Proceedings of the IFIP Congress* (1962): 567–569.

ERLI72   Erlinger, M. *Microprogramming and its Use in an Extensible Processor,* report no. UCLA-ENG-7230. Los Angeles: Computer Science Department, University of California, April 1972.

FLYN67   Flynn, M. J., and MacLaren, M. D. "Microprogramming Revisited." *Proceedings of the ACM National Meeting,* 1967: 457–464.

FLYN71A   Flynn, M. J. *Control Through Microprogramming*. Grenoble: NATO International Advanced Summer Institute on Microprogramming, August 30–September 10, 1971.

FLYN71C   Flynn, M. J., and Rosin, R. I. "Microprogramming: An Introduction and a Viewpoint." *IEEE Transactions on Computers* C-20, no. 7 (July 1971): 727–731.

GARL71   Gardner, L. *Automated Production of Soft Interpreters For Disk Memory Systems*. Grenoble: NATO International Advanced Summer Institute on Microprogramming, August 30–September 10, 1971.

GARP71   Gardner, P. L. "Functional Memory and its Microprogramming Implications." *IEEE Transactions on Computers* C-20, no. 7 (July 1971): 764–775.

GRAS62   Grasselli, A. "The Design of Program-Modifiable Micro-Programmed Control Units." *IRE Transactions on Electronic Computers* EC-11, no. 6 (June 1962): 334–339.

GSCH67   Gschwind, H. W. *Design of Digital Computers*. New York: Springer-Verlag, 1967, pp. 379–387.

HOFF71   Hoff, G. *Design of Microprogrammed Control for General Purpose Processors*. Grenoble: NATO International Advanced Summer Institute on Microprogramming, August 30–September 10, 1971.

HOPK70   Hopkins, W. C. "A Multi-Emulator Operating System for a Microprogrammable Computer." *Preprints of the ACM 3rd Annual Workshop on Microprogramming,* October 1970.

HOUS73   House, David L. "Micro Level Architecture in Minicomputer Design." *Computer Design* 12, no. 10 (October 1973): 75–80.

HPCM72   Hewlett-Packard Company. *Microprogramming Guide, HP2100 Computer,* no. 5951-3028 (February 1972).

HPCM74   Hewlett-Packard Company. *Microprogramming 21MX Computers: Operating and Reference Manual,* no. 02108-90008 (August 1974).

HUSS67   Husson, S. S. "Microprogramming Manual for the IBM System/360 Model 50." *IBM Technical Report,* no. TR 00.1479-1 (October 2, 1967).

HUSS70   Husson, S. S. *Microprogramming: Principles and Practices*. Englewood-Cliffs, N.J.: Prentice-Hall, 1970.

HUSS71   Husson, S. S. *Principles of Microprogramming*. Grenoble: NATO International Advanced Summer Institute on Microprogramming, August 30–September 10, 1971.

IBM71   International Business Machines Corporation. *An Introduction to Microprogramming,* no. GF20-0385-0 (December 1971).

INTL75   Intel Corporation. *Schottky Bipolar LSI Microcomputer Set: 3001 Microprogram Control Unit and 3002 Central Processing Element,* 1975.

INTR74   Interdata Incorporated. *Model 8/32 Micro-Program Description*, no. 05-058A15 (December 1974).

JONE72   Jones, L. H., et al. "An Annotated Bibliography on Microprogramming, Late 1969–Early 1972." *SIGMICRO Newsletter* 3 (July 1972): 34–55.

JONE73   Jones, L. H., and Carvin, K. "An Annotated Bibliography of Microprogramming II: Early 1972–Early 1973." *SIGMICRO Newsletter* 4 (July 1973): 7–18.

JONE74   Jones, L. H., and Merwin, R. E. "Trends in Microprogramming: A Second Reading." *IEEE Transactions on Computers*, August 1974: 754–759.

LAWS71   Lawson, H. W., and Smith, B. K. "Functional Characteristics of a Multilingual Processor." *IEEE Transactions on Computers* C-20, no. 7 (July 1971): 732–742.

LEIS71   Leis, C. T. "Microprogramming Features of 16-bit Mini." *Preprints of the ACM 4th Annual Workshop on Microprogramming.* Santa Cruz: University of California, September 13–14, 1971.

LESS71   Lesser, V. R. *An Introduction to the Direct Emulation of Control Structures by a Parallel Micro-Computer*, report no. STAN-CS-71-191. Stanford, Calif.: Computer Science Department, Stanford University, January 1971.

LESS72   Lesser, V. R. *Dynamic Control Structures and Their Use in Emulation*, report no. GS-309. Stanford, Calif.: Computer Science Department, Stanford University, October 1972.

LEVY65   Levy, L. S. *State of the Art of Microprogramming*, report no. TOR-469(5710-01)-1. El Segundo, Calif.: Aerospace Corporation, April 15, 1965.

LEVY73   Levy, J. V. *Computing with Multiple Microprocessors*, SLAC report no. 161. Stanford, Calif.: Stanford Linear Accelerator Center, April 1973.

MCCL71   McClure, R. M. *Parallelism in Microprogrammed Controls*. Grenoble: NATO International Advanced Summer Institute on Microprogramming, August 30–September 10, 1971.

MCKE67   McKeeman, W. M. "Language Directed Computer Design." *Proceedings of the AFIPS Conference* 31(FJCC) (1967): 413–417.

MICR71   Microdata Corporation. *Microprogramming Handbook*, 1971.

MICR74   Microdata Corporation. *Microdata 3200 Computer, Product Information Sheet*, 1974.

NANO74   Nanodata Corporation. *QM-1 Hardware Level User's Manual.* 2d ed., rev. August 31, 1974.

NOGU71   Noguez, G. L. M. "A Standardized Microprogram Sequencing Control with a Push-Down Storage." *Preprints of the ACM 5th Annual Workshop on Microprogramming*, 1972: 66–71.

OPLE67   Opler, A. "Fourth Generation Software." *Datamation* 13, no. 1 (January 1967): 22–24.

PATZ67   Patzer, W. J., and Vandling, G. C. "Systems Implications of Microprogramming." *Computer Design* 6, no. 12 (December 1967): 62–66.

RAKO71   Rakocsi, L. L. *Microprogramming the MLP-900 as a Fourth Generation Computer System.* Grenoble: NATO International Advanced Summer Institute on Microprogramming, August 30–September 10, 1971.

RAMA70   Ramamoorthy, C. V., and Tsuchiya, M. "A Study of User-Microprogrammable Computers." *Proceedings of the AFIPS Conference* 36(SJCC) (1970): 165–181.

RAMA72   Ramamoorthy, C. V., and Tsuchiya, M. "Analysis of Microprogrammed Processor Design Trade-Offs." *COMPCON 72,* 1972: 111–114.

RATT74   Rattner, Justin; Cornet, J.; and Hoff, M. E., Jr. "Bipolar LSI Computing Elements Usher in New Era of Digital Design." *Electronics,* September 5, 1974: 89–96.

REDF71   Redfield, S. R. "A Study of Microprogrammed Processors: A Medium Sized Microprogrammed Processor." *IEEE Transactions on Computers* C-20, no. 7 (July 1971): 743–750.

REIG72   Reigel, E. W.; Faber, U.; and Fisher, D. A. "The Interpreter–A Microprogrammable Building Block System." *Proceedings of the AFIPS Conference* 40(SJCC) (1972): 705–723.

ROSI69A   Rosin, R. F. "Contemporary Concepts of Microprogramming and Emulation." *Computing Surveys* 1, no. 4 (December 1969): 197–212.

ROSI69B   Rosin, R. F. *MPP–A Tool for Teaching and Research in Microprogramming,* no. PN-3. Buffalo, N Y Department of Computer Science, State University of New York, April 1969.

ROSI71   Rosin, R. F.; Frieder, G.; and Eckhouse, R., Jr. "An Environment for Research in Microprogramming and Emulation." *Communications of the ACM* 15, no. 8 (August 1972): 748–760 (1st published in 1971).

SAAL70   Saal, H. *Microprogram Organization for the Execution of a Wide-Spectrum Higher Level Language,* no. SLAC-CGTM-85. Stanford, Calif.: Stanford University Press, February 1970.

SALI73   Salisbury, A. B. *The Evaluation of Microprogram Implemented Emulators,* no. 60. Stanford, Calif.: Digital Systems Laboratory, Stanford University, July 1973.

SCHN65   Schnabel, D. L. *The Design of Processor Controls Using a Read-Only Storage,* no. TROO.1318. Poughkeepsie, N.Y.: IBM Systems Development Division, August 30, 1965.

SIGM74   SIGMICROprogramming Newsletter, Association for Computing Machinery. *Microprogramming Bibliography 1951–Early 1974,* special issue, September 1974.

SMIT59   Smith, C. V. L. *Electronic Digital Computers.* New York: McGraw-Hill, 1959.

STAN70   Standard Computer Corporation. *IC-9000 Processor Functional Description,* form 9001-3, undated.

TOMP74   Tompkins, Howard E. *Microprogrammer's Manual for the Microdata 3200,* manuscript ed., June 1974.

ⴑSUC72   Tsuchiya, M. and Ramamoorthy, C. V. *Design of a Multilevel Microprogrammable Computer and a High Level Microprogramming Language,* no. 135. Austin, Texas: Electronics Research Center, University of Texas, August 15, 1972.

TUCK67   Tucker, S. G. "Microprogram Control for System/360." *IBM Systems Journal* 6, no. 4 (1967): 222–241.

TUCK71   Tucker, A. B., and Flynn, M. J. "Dynamic Microprogramming: Processor Organization and Programming." *Communications of the ACM* 14, no. 4 (April 1971): 240–250.

VAUG72   Vaugham, R. F., and Collins, R. A. "On Computer Architecture, Software Portability and Microprogramming." *Computer Architecture News* 1, no. 4 (October 1972): 14–15.

VARM72   Varian Data Machines. *Varian Microprogramming Guide,* preliminary ed., no. 98A9906071, December 1972.

WEST75   Western Digital Corporation. *MCP 1600 Microprocessor Product Description,* preliminary ed.

WILK51   Wilkes, M. V. "The Best Way to Design an Automatic Calculating Machine." *Proceedings of the Manchester University Computer Inaugural Conference.* London: Ferranti, July 1951.

WILK53   Wilkes, M. V., and Stringer, J. B. "Microprogramming and the Design of the Control Circuits in an Electronic Digital Computer." *Proceedings of the Cambridge Philosophical Society* 49, part 2 (April 1953): 230–238.

WILK69   Wilkes, M. V. "The Growth of Interest in Microprogramming: A Literature Survey." *Computing Surveys* 1, no. 3 (September 1969): 139–145.

WILK72   Wilkes, M. V. "The Use of a Writable Control Memory In a Multiprogramming Environment." *Preprints of the ACM 5th Annual Workshop on Microprogramming,* 1972: 62–65.

WILN72   Wilner, W. T. "Design of the B1700." *Proceedings of the AFIPS Conference* 41(FJCC) (1972): 489–497

Index